Men of Spirit
Men of Sports

Wally Carew

Ambassador Books, Inc.
Worcester • Massachusetts

ISBN: 1-929039-00-X
Library of Congress Catalog Card Number: 99-067279

Published in the United States by Ambassador Books, Inc.
91 Prescott Street, Worcester, Massachusetts 01605
(800) 577-0909

Printed in the United States.
For current information about all titles from Ambassador Books, Inc.,
visit our website at: www.ambassadorbooks.com.

Contents

Dedication

This book is dedicated to my family, all the Carews and all the Healys; to my wife, Mary Rose; to my four stepchildren and four grandchildren; to my wife's family, the Michalowskis; to every teammate and opponent I played with and against; and with the utmost of gratitude to Father William R. Anderson, the retired pastor of St. Camillus Parish in Arlington, Massachusetts. Father Anderson is my closest friend and spiritual father.

Appreciation

F irst of all, this book would have remained no more than an idea were it not for the love, understanding, encouragement, total support and patience of my wife, Mary Rose.

I lived the first forty-five years of my life without her. How I managed, only my guardian angel can say. Thankfully, the past eleven years with her have been better. Just plain better for a thousand reasons. She is an avid reader, a talented artist, and I trust her and her opinions. I submit no work for publication, at any level, until she has read it.

How she has managed to put up with me, which includes my obsessive personality—so much a part of this writer—I will never know.

Secondly, I am grateful to my editor, Gerry Goggins, and the staff at Ambassador Books, particularly Jennifer Goggins and Sister Susan Terkanian, CTC. They care about quality, but they care even more about people. Never once did they complain about my habit of telephoning "to check on every last detail."

As for editor Gerry, he stroked me when I needed it and hit me over the head with a hammer when necessary. I respect him as a professional. But even more important, he is a friend. Most of our work on this book was done over the telephone. Once I said to him: "Why don't I just drive out to Worcester and let's get this thing done!" His response? "If two Irishmen like you and me tried to work in the same office, we might end up killing each other!"

Next question?

I want to extend a special thank you to Jimmy Kerr, Harry Agganis's best friend. It was through him, that I came to feel that I knew Harry personally.

There are others I want to thank. They include Dana Pierce, Bruce Woodworth, Danner DeStephano, my family—my mother, Catherine Healy Carew, and my brothers and sisters, Tommy, Mary Judith, Christine Marie, Jimmy, and Dennis. They are part of me and much of who they are played a major role in all that went into this book; the trio of archivists for the Archdiocese of Boston—Robert Johnson-Lally, Phyllis Danehy, and Mary Lou Jacobs; Joyce Woodman of the Concord Library; Mrs. Marguerite Dalton, Jimmy Dalton, Kathleen Dalton Nannicelli, and James Hancock.

Getting Grounded

T he idea that led me to put this book together goes back almost fifty years, to when, as a boy, I used to stop at the train depot in West Concord and listen to the old timers share the stories of their lives. It was spellbinding.

I have always been passionate about sports, fascinated by people, and intrigued by stories. After he put us to bed, my father, Walter Sr., an English teacher and coach, would read to my younger brother and me. It was a toasty feeling being bundled in bed with the wind howling and the snow blowing outside, listening to my dad read excerpts from the novel *Snowbound*. I can still feel the excitement and the combination of warmth and chill.

For as long as I can remember, the Catholic faith has been the center of my life. Thanks to the efforts of my parents, relatives, family friends and a long list of priests and nuns, I received a solid spiritual foundation.

I grew up late and my teens and twenties were difficult, exasperating years. It took time for me to realize the truth about myself and about life.

I have always been wild about sports, even at an early age. As the first-born of a high school football and baseball coach, I was privileged. Every day was an opportunity to explore the inner sanctum of athletics and experience intimacies that other boys my age were denied. Over the years, I took a lot of mental notes, savoring each moment and every detail. The special sights, sounds, and smells of those years dominated my youth in a wonderful way.

Experience is a true teacher, and ordinary happenings produce the best material. I learned to field grounders by bouncing a tennis ball off the front steps of my grandparents' home in Medford, Massachusetts. They lived on a hill, and if I booted a grounder, I had to chase the ball to the bottom of the hill. I didn't want to climb and reclimb the hill, so I didn't boot many.

How can anyone forget the travails of playing Little League baseball? It was that awkward period in life prior to adolescence. Heck, one of my closest friends sucked his thumb between pitches while he patrolled the outfield.

It was ironic that many of the biggest Little League baseball stars, just a few years later, failed to make the varsity baseball team in high school.

To me, it seemed that the worst coaches in the world descended like monsters on the Little League baseball scene. Most knew nothing about the game. They had never played marbles, let alone baseball.

As far as I am concerned, Little League baseball ruined the game. Kids no longer played on their own. Adults took the fun out of the sport. Today, baseball, at all levels, has slipped badly. Where have all the players with strong throwing arms gone? What happened to baseball instincts that are only acquired after years of repetition?

I grew up during the late 1940s and the 1950s in historic Concord, Massachusetts. Back then, we had time to be young. Boys were boys and girls were girls. No one thought, let alone tried, to neuter the sexes. We probably had as many problems as kids do today, but life did not come at us so fast. Life as an adult was something to be lived in the future, and there was ample time to play and to dream.

Mischief was a part of being young. Take, for example, Andy Peterson. He was a top bowler and a talented softball pitcher whose windmill delivery whipped the ball across home plate. During the day, he drove the Cushman Bakery truck that made the rounds of our neighborhood. While he made deliveries to homes, my friend and I stealthily slipped around to the back of the truck and liberated him of extra boxes of goodies, such as cupcakes, cookies, tarts and brownies. Long ago, I asked God to forgive us. The forgiveness that I received is complete now that I have gone public.

Dad worked and my mother took care of the home and everyone in it, including me, my younger brothers and sisters—Tommy, Mary Judith, Christine Marie, Jimmy and Dennis, plus the dogs and cats. Mom sacrificed much, including her interests in art, horses and the theater, just to raise a family. Our family became her entire life. That may not have been what was best for her or for the rest of us. But that is the way it was. It was her choice. Despite their flaws, I am certain that my parents based their decisions on their love for God and what they believed was best for their six children.

When I think of my youth, I remember seemingly insignificant events: looking forward to eating spaghetti and meatballs every Monday night; the day my father had a pole, backboard and basket put up in the back yard so I could shoot hoops morning, noon and night; watching Pinky Lee, The Lone Ranger and the Mickey Mouse Club during the early days of black and white television; being allowed to stay up extra late so I could watch Heavyweight Champion Rocky Marciano defend his title; the family ritual of making popcorn on Friday nights—of course, my father always had the biggest bowl; playing tackle football on grass that sloped along the side of our home on Pleasant Street; covering every inch of my bedroom walls with tacked-up color photos from *Sport Magazine*; and the Christmas morning a Collie puppy was among the gifts under the tree.

I always knew that someday I would write this book. Many of the stories were written after I decided to write about sports from a Catholic-Christian perspective. When I think of the people and events in this book, I am reminded of the spirit of the Army-Navy game, the legend that is Notre Dame, the fire of Mike Ditka, the faithfulness of former Red Sox manager Joe Morgan, the style of Bob Cousy, the perseverance of Red Schoendienst, the strength of Jimmy O'Brien, the dignity of Stan Musial, the depth of Roger Staubach, the loyalty of Admiral Tom Lynch, the wisdom of Bowie Kuhn, the faith of Bishop Jeremiah Minihan, the giftedness of Mickey Mantle, the humility of Gerry Faust, the courage of Jackie Robinson, the character of Jim Lonborg, the joyfulness of Ernie Banks, and the heroism of my late teammate Eddie Dalton.

Despite much work, I knew intuitively that something was missing, and that something was my story. The book did not come together until I wrote honestly about my own experiences. Once I did, I discovered tremendous joy.

Thank God.

Wally Carew
March 19, 1999
the Feast of St. Joseph

Part One

Sports Central

The Angelus

The ringing of the Angelus haunted me as a boy. The sound of the bells chiming from the bell tower of Our Lady Help of Christians Church filled the streets of the town. Their solemn tones reached the Fowler Memorial Library at Main and Church Streets and cascaded across the street to the Union Church.

The bells' sound stretched down Church Street to the village of West Concord, which historians called the Junction. That was where "Mr. Amateur Baseball"—Barry Higgins, a postal worker, local newspaper columnist and unofficial mayor—held forth. And the ringing of the Angelus could be heard a mile away at Percy Rideout Playground.

"Bong...Bong...Bong...Bong..." It rang three times every day—at six in the morning, at noon, and at six at night.

Occasionally, the recording of the Angelus became stuck, and Jack Daly, the sexton, had to climb up the winding stairs that led to the bell tower and adjust the timer. If for some reason you didn't hear the bells, the natural ebb and flow of life somehow seemed jarred.

From as far back as I can remember, I was moved by the mystical beauty of the bells announcing the Annunciation. Clearly, the sound was different. It was mellow and rich—not like the train whistle which was distant, yet made you feel cozy, especially late at night when you were bundled up in bed. And it was totally unlike the fire whistle which was harsh and jolting.

At six P.M., people who worked in Boston got off the train at the depot in the village and walked home. Many climbed the hill and passed Our Lady Help of Christians as the solemn yet joyful bells announced the Good News.

In the spring, May or early June, dressed in a Little League uniform, I would head to a game at Rideout Playground. As I passed the front entrance to the church, directly below a statue of Our Lady, the Angelus rang so loudly that I almost had to cover my ears.

Some nights, particularly if I was in a wistful mood, I would stop and listen to the bells. The sound was both comforting and perplexing as if it gave rise to an unanswered question. In my small world during the early 1950s, there was no other sound that compared to the ringing of the Angelus.

As an Irish-American altar boy, attending Catholic grammar school, I was accustomed to sounds and silence that draw attention to God. Many of us made visits to the chapel and prayed before the Blessed Sacrament on the way out the door to recess. Being an altar boy had its own rewards, too—like being dismissed from school to serve at funeral Masses. Father Tom Morgan, newly ordained, was a curate at Our Lady's. A rugged, handsome man with unruly black hair, he was every altar boy's hero. He drove a 1951 black Chevy. Periodically, one or more of the doors became stuck and to ride in the car you had to climb through a rolled-down window.

Sometimes unannounced, Father Morgan would appear at Rose Hawthorne Elementary School and barge into the middle of Bible history class. As the class jumped to its feet, the teacher, a Sister of the Holy Union, surprised but hardly flustered by the sudden intrusion, would give him a slight bow.

"Good morning, Father," the nun would say.

"Say good morning to Father," she would order.

"Good morning, Father," repeated the class.

Father Morgan would whisper something to the nun and she would call out my name and the name of a classmate, Peter Dalton. "Walter and Peter come here this minute. Father needs both of you to serve a funeral Mass. You are to go with him and he will bring you directly back to school."

As soon as we spotted Father, Peter and I knew why he was there and both of us started smiling like cats who had eaten canaries, but once in front of the class, we put on our serious faces for the benefit of sister and our not-so-lucky classmates.

You could hear a pin drop as we followed Father Morgan down the school corridor and through two sets of double doors that led to the schoolyard. Outside, Peter and I would scream with delight and do a little dance.

After the funeral Mass, Father Morgan always took Peter and me for a strawberry or vanilla shake. Before returning us to school, he gave each of us a dollar despite our brief and unsuccessful protests.

Father Morgan was an avid sports fan. At six feet, two hundred pounds, he regularly participated in pick-up basketball games at the Thoreau School gym. A left-hander, he was not known for a delicate shooting touch. He played basketball like it was roller derby. Working up a good lather, he dripped sweat as he crashed into bodies and sent them flying. If there was a referee, he would have fouled out in short order.

The pastor was Father Louis Kern, a good priest and a kind man who stuttered severely and struggled through each and every homily. As kids, we respected Father Kern, a short, round, older man with thinning hair, but Father Morgan was our priest, a knight who wore a black cassock, except when he played basketball in a navy blue sweat suit with the sleeves pushed up to his elbows.

After a few years, Father Morgan was transferred to another parish. After he left, the village of West Concord did not seem the same. He was missed and so was his 1951 black Chevy rattletrap.

During the early 1950s, West Concord was a typical suburban American town. In the summer, breakfast consisted of cold cereal, milk and toast. Keds—high-topped black sneakers—dungarees and pull-over short-sleeve shirts with horizontal stripes was the uniform of the day. And baseball was thought about, talked about, and played from morning until night.

There were only a few stores in the village—Prendergast Market, the West Concord Super Market—better known as Mandrioli's—the drug store, where a pretty, middle-age woman named Grace Collins fixed the best cherry Cokes in town, a barber shop, Condon's Liquor Store, the post office, Hays Shoe Store, the West Concord 5 & 10, and one or two others. There was also a train depot, where the old timers congregated and reminisced. It was there where I heard about the horse and buggy days, the horrors of fighting in World War I, and the exciting times prior to the 1920s when Babe Ruth played for the Red Sox and lived a mere six miles away in Sudbury.

"The Babe used to pass through here," they would recall. "We'd see him every winter. He had many hang-outs around here."

West Concord Junction had its share of characters. Charlie Lombardo ran the barber shop. Trim and well-dressed, he always wore a white shirt and tie. He was a stately-looking man with a head of full, white hair which he meticulously combed so not a single strand was ever out of place. He and his wife went to the 11:30 Mass at Our Lady's every Sunday morning. He smoked Camels, one after another. Charlie was an earthy guy and he could be crusty at times. But he was a gentleman, always courteous when mothers parked their boys in his barbershop.

Back then, there was only one haircut of choice for boys. It was called "The Charlie Special"—otherwise known as a whiffle. No scissors were required. Just the shears. Starting at the hairline above the forehead, Charlie "The Barber" moved his shears over your head in a straight line all the way down to the base of the neck, just above your shoulders. After about eight repetitions, being extra careful when he got close to your ears, it was finished. He would remove the sheet that reached to your chin, shake the cut hair onto the floor, splash Witch hazel on the back of your neck, and sprinkle a little powder on you. He would get the $1.25 your mother had given you, and out into the summer sun you went, practically bald but sure that it would be at least a month before you would encounter Charlie and his shears again.

Brothers John and Tom ran Prendergast Market, a store not much bigger than the average sitting room. Meat was their specialty. The market took orders over the telephone and delivered to homes. Groceries were scarce and only the bare necessities were stocked on very lean-looking shelves. The selection of candy was meager at best—although the Prendergast brothers did carry baseball cards.

John was a huge, broad-shouldered man who weighed close to three hundred pounds. As a youth, he had been a standout offensive and defensive tackle in football. As large as he was on the outside, he was a lamb on the inside, a meek soul with a sweet disposition. He was filled with mirth. At Christmas, he dressed up as Santa Claus for the kids. Brother Tom was his opposite. As thin as a rail, he wore wire-rimmed glasses. He was as kind as his brother but much more serious and subdued. They also ran an insurance business, and the Prendergasts were highly regarded in the community.

The stores in the village gave my best friend, Ricky Loughlin, and me two cents for every soda pop bottle we turned in. Regularly, we combed the railroad tracks looking for empty bottles, always found a supply and turned them in for money to buy baseball cards, at five cents per pack.

The most striking card I ever owned was from a 1953 or 1954 series—I think Topps put it out. The card featured a real-life, glossy color photo of Walter "Hoot" Evers, a solid American League outfielder who hit .278 in twelve big-league seasons with the Tigers, Red Sox, Indians, Giants and

Orioles. The card showed Evers when he played with the Red Sox, kneeling in the on-deck circle with a pair of bats resting on his right shoulder at the old Briggs Stadium in Detroit. It was a beauty, a true classic. I had hundreds of baseball cards, some dating as far back as 1949, like the ones I saved of Earl Torgeson and Sibby Sisti, former members of the Boston Braves.

I even had a Mickey Mantle 1951 rookie card. In vintage shape, that card is worth a lot of money today. I also had a 1949 pro football card of Pete Pihos, the great end who played for the Philadelphia Eagles. Unfortunately, when I left home to enter the Army, my mother trashed my baseball and football card collections.

There wasn't much excitement in West Concord during the 1950s. Sadly, one time an elderly lady committed suicide by throwing herself in front of a train. There were a couple of huge fires, one that leveled a wood-working company and another that destroyed Our Lady's Church. That was truly sad. I remember standing in the dark of night and shivering in the dead of winter watching the flames light up the sky. "How could Our Lady let this happen?" I asked myself. Looking back, it seemed as if Richard Cardinal Cushing, Archbishop and builder extraordinaire, saw to it that Our Lady's was rebuilt almost overnight although the work took several months.

One time, the Junction came alive when word spread that a celebrity had stopped at Prendergast Market. As kids, we rushed down to the village to investigate. Someone said that the celebrity was Billy Cox, the glue-gloved Brooklyn Dodgers' third baseman and one of the Boys of Summer. As it turned out, all the fuss was over not *Billy* Cox, but *Wally* Cox, the gnomish, bespectacled actor who played "Mr. Peepers" during the early days of black and white television. Wally Cox was hardly Billy Cox, so the excitement quickly fizzled, at least for my friends and me.

During the fall, we played tackle football anywhere we could—in back-yards, open lots, behind the church and in schoolyards. For awhile, we played behind Our Lady's until we dug up the grass so badly that Father Kern shooed us away for good.

It was rough and tumble football. No one wore pads and only a few were fortunate enough to have helmets. I had a gold-painted leather helmet, a relic of Concord High football past. My father, the coach, brought it home for me. Inside, it smelled of sweat. But I loved it and wore it proudly.

Once playing behind Our Lady's, I tackled a classmate and broke his leg. His name was Paul McClure, a tall, slim boy who was a superb student.

He wore penny loafers, was a preppy dresser and all the girls had crushes on him. After he was injured, his mother did not speak to me for months. The last I heard of him he was a border guard in the Southwest. Then several years ago, someone told me that he had died. I remember him with fondness.

Except for McClure's broken leg, there were few serious injuries—just bruises, burns, headaches and the daily bloody noses. In terms of ability, some were better than others, and a few were tougher than the rest. As for raw speed, one boy was the swiftest, a regular greyhound. His name was Dicky Francis. I hated him because he was not only faster, but also shiftier than anyone else, including me. I loved to play against him, just to try and tackle him. Most of the time, I ended up flat on my stomach after he skipped past me and dashed into the distance, off on a touchdown run.

Looking up, I watched him running away. Often, I pounded both fists on the ground and hollered, "I'll get you next time, Francis!" More than scoring a touchdown myself, I savored the few times I was able to drive a shoulder into Francis—the human speedball—and knock him to the ground. In high school, Dicky Francis was a speedy scatback. He was just as difficult to tackle then as he had been as a boy. In high school, we were teammates and played in the same backfield. He usually did the running and I blocked.

Speaking of teammates, three of my all-time favorites are Bobby Windheim, Bernie Kelley and Billy Napoli. Windheim, a gentle giant, was one of the biggest (over two hundred pounds) and fastest players on the high school squad. He was a fullback and he exploded for two, long touchdown runs (both fifty yards or more) in his final game as a senior, Thanksgiving morning 1960. That day, we crushed arch-rival Lexington, 30-6. He later became the manager of a liquor store in Concord.

Kelley, the son of the former Concord Police Chief, was a gangly guard who had the trainer wrap him in layers of tape so he would appear bigger. He ultimately become a computer whiz, a musician and song writer.

Napoli also was a guard. He weighed 135 pounds, 130 of which was heart. His older brother, Charlie, weighed about 230 and was a standout lineman. All Billy lacked was Charlie's body. A jack-of-all-trades, Billy has never given less than one hundred percent in anything.

I must mention Kenneth "Kit" Harris. Blond and blue-eyed, he had a body like a Viking god, a six feet two inches, 200 pound man-child. He was fast, too, although he was not naturally tough. Through determination, he made himself into a capable football player. A straight-A student, my father once called him "the finest student I ever taught." After high school, Kit matriculated at Princeton. Sadly, he died suddenly before the end of his freshman year. I have never forgotten him. He was special, both on and off the field, and he was kind to everyone regardless of their social or classroom standing.

Those are memories of high school football, a step above sandlot football. I remember one pickup football game in particular. It was January 1, 1954. Snow was on the ground. It was bitter cold, but I organized a tackle football game in the Francis family yard, one of our favorite places to play tackle football. Later that same day, Michigan State and UCLA played in the Rose Bowl [Michigan State won, 28-20]. After we had split into opposing squads, I declared that our team was Michigan State, so I could make believe I was Billy Wells, the star running back for the Spartans. "You guys can be the UCLA Bruins," I said to friends on the "other" team. I was excited about the chance to stage a fantasy Rose Bowl. It was blustery outside, but that thought alone made me feel toasty on the inside. I always had a vivid imagination.

Regularly, we made up games, like "Goal Line Stand" for instance. Usually there were five on a side. Sometimes more. We drew a line across the dirt near the street—the goal line. Five on defense and five on offense. We placed the football one yard from the goal line. The offense had to pound the football into the imaginary end zone, and the five on defense had to dig in and stop them. It was great. There was a lot of hooting and hollering. Many pileups, stacks of bodies, heated arguments that sometimes almost came to blows, but one heck of a good time. Among the participants were me, my younger brother Tommy, the Francis brothers, the Alden brothers, the Viscariello brothers, Ricky Loughlin, Billy Walsh, Jack Humphrey, Johnny Devlin, Paul Delaney, Johnny Daly and others.

It was dark and time to head home for dinner when the goal line stand game ended. I always carried a football everywhere I went. On my way home, I stood under a street light, threw the football up in the air, caught it, and pretended I was Howard "Hopalong" Cassady, old Number 40 of the Ohio State Buckeyes. Then, I zig-zagged my way home, pretending to be Cassady as the ex-Buckeye great returned a punt for a touchdown.

Those were special days. All things seemed possible and life was innocent and uncomplicated growing up in a suburban hamlet seventeen miles west of Boston during the Fabulous 1950s. There were problems—lots of them. But it was an era when people actually blushed.

Thanksgiving Day, 1948

Assistant Concord High School football coach Walter Carew, Sr. is carried off the field after a smashing 28-0 victory over archrival Lexington High School.

A Large Shadow

He was an All-Scholastic quarterback. He was a three-sport star in college. He was a war hero—an Army Infantry Captain who was wounded twice in the Battle of the Bulge. He was a pillar of the Church who truly loved his faith, the darling and baby of a proud Irish family of fifteen children. He was a model citizen and the most patriotic man I ever met. He was a snappy dresser, always neat and disciplined. He did not smoke, seldom drank anything stronger than root beer and never swore, unless you consider "For God's sake" taking the name of the Lord in vain.

I don't.

By nature, he was a reserved, shy man. His reticence, however, did not extend to infants and toddlers. My father was putty around babies. He loved young children, his or anybody else's. He picked them up, made funny faces to make them giggle and covered their soft, delicate faces with kisses.

That was one side of my dad: warm, tender and loving.

He had an appetite like a truck driver or a longshoreman, yet he kept his weight under control. Darn near perfectly. He stood five feet ten inches and weighed around one hundred and seventy pounds. In his sixties, he played competitive basketball, more than holding his own against men much younger and teenagers, many of them bona fide high school stars.

You knew he had been a great athlete, just by the way he carried himself. He was a strong, graceful man, even when he stooped to pick up a newspaper or a baby. He stood as straight as a soldier, forever and a day a true military veteran. He came from an Army background. Two of his older brothers, John and Larry, despite just elementary school educations, somehow managed to become generals.

He was passionate about parades, and he traveled anywhere and everywhere to hear a marching band. When I was very young, he gave me a bat, ball, baseball glove and a tiny American flag, but not necessarily in that

Courtesy of the Carew family

It was in the blood.
Walter Carew, Sr., the author's father, is number 54 in this 1935 photo of the Medford High School Mustangs. Future fellow Concord High assistant football coach, John O'Connell, is number 30.

order. I grew up watching parades with him and listening to the big sound of marching bands, the more brass the better. He sobbed uncontrollably on the first Patriots Day that he was too ill and feeble to march in the annual parade.

He and I played countless games of one-on-one basketball. I had my own abilities, particularly when it came to "shooting the rock," as Dick Vitale would say; yet I never beat him. Not even once.

In 1940, he graduated from St. Bonaventure University with a Bachelor of Arts degree in English. Later, he earned a master's degree in education from Boston College. He was voted "The Ideal Bonaventure Man" by the senior class. Were it not for the war, he would have played professional baseball. The Brooklyn Dodgers were hot on his trail, as were other teams. He was a shortstop and center fielder who could do it all—hit for average and power, and throw, field and run. He was not blessed with blinding speed, but he was shifty, heady, and quick, and he had the finest instincts of any athlete I have ever observed. Everyone told me he was a natural and I was awed by how much ability he actually possessed.

Sadly, he never had a chance to play for the Dodgers or any of the other big league teams. World War II ruined that. It robbed him of his peak years as an athlete. By the time he was discharged from the Army, he was too old to begin playing kids' games for money. Plus, he had a wife and young son—me.

The dream of playing sports in the big time evaporated in the smoke from a global war. So he did the next best thing. He became a teacher and a coach, teaching English and coaching football and baseball.

He never made it to Cooperstown, although given a chance, I know he could have. Nevertheless, he is enshrined in five Halls of Fame, two as a player and three as a coach. In 1988, he was inducted into the St. Bonaventure University Athletic Hall of Fame. He loved the Bonnies—the rustic campus located in Olean, New York, the color brown, the whole deal. He was inspired by St. Francis and the Franciscans. He was the only one in his family to graduate from college, so that induction was extra special. As a youth, his mother had wanted him to become a priest, and that pressure may have caused him guilt, perhaps, subconsciously.

He cared deeply about every boy he coached and every student he taught. Two of his all-time favorite student-athletes, Jim McKenna and John Pierce, followed in his footsteps. They enrolled at St. Bonaventure and played college football for the Bonnies. Following college and a stint in the Army, Pierce even traveled the extra yard; he studied for the priesthood and was ordained not just a priest, but a Franciscan priest. Today, he is Father John Pierce, OFM. My dad was their father, they his sons. Like my father, McKenna and Pierce quickly became my heroes, too. Often, they baby-sat for me and my younger siblings.

I was his oldest child, his first born son, his namesake, and he, Walter R. Carew Sr., was a giant figure in my eyes.

How in the world does a son live up to such a legacy?

He doesn't.

The biggest mistake I made was that, for years, I truly believed I had to try.

Trying meant failing. Then, when the mountain appeared too tall to view the top, I stopped trying. I rebelled. I lowered my sights and slipped into a free-fall that began around the time I became a teenager and lasted until I was thirty. Through the grace of God, the bottom became not the end, but the beginning. It was there that I found someone I had never known—myself.

My father coached me in two sports, football and baseball. He was an assistant football coach and the head baseball coach. He became the head football coach the season after I graduated, a position he held for a decade. After he retired, he was replaced by one of his assistant coaches, Al Robichaud, who coached Concord to its only Super Bowl championship.

In fact, however, my father had been the head football coach for years without the title. Head coach Bernie Megin was in declining health and had been for a long time. He was absent more than he was present. In his absence, dad ran the show and no one doubted it.

In football, I played defensive end, linebacker and halfback. I was the only sophomore starter on the varsity. At five feet six inches, one hundred and sixty pounds, I was a tough, solid blocker and tackler—when I wanted to be. There were days when I didn't give a hoot and fluffed off which infuriated my father. One look from him told me how he felt—disgusted, embarrassed, humiliated, disgraced.

In my junior year, I went so far as to quit. I faked an injury. I came out of the game and did not return. I fooled everyone except him. He knew I was faking, that I was not hurt, that I was in one of my "I don't feel like playing moods." If looks could have killed, I would have died on that warm early Saturday afternoon in October 1960, in Reading, Massachusetts, in front of three thousand people.

He was hurt. I was hurting, too, but not physically. Looking back, what wounded me the most, deep down in my soul, was his reaction. He did not speak to me for what seemed like weeks. Not one single word. Whenever he came home, I rushed up to my room so I would not have to face him.

In baseball, I was a catcher. Catching was as natural to me as splashing Aqua Velva on my face or combing my teenage hair. I also had a powerful rifle arm. Years after my playing days were over, my father was still convinced that "I could have made the big leagues." He often mouthed those sentiments to others, including my mother, who repeated them to me. I have often thought about that. "Maybe if I had been more focused, more steady," I would tell myself, "I could have had a shot."

Truthfully, I think my father was transferring his abilities and ambitions to me, while wrestling with the frustration surrounding his own aborted athletic career. I am short, below average height, and during my era the days of stubby catchers like Yogi Berra and Clint Courtney were dwindling fast. Big, tall men, like Carlton Fisk and Johnny Bench, were the catchers of the future. Plus, I was a weak hitter, a fact attributed to poor eyesight which has gotten worse as I have gotten older.

I was the starting catcher on the varsity baseball team when I was only a freshman. We had good teams and made the state tournament, led by a fire-balling southpaw pitcher named Dave Niemi, who eventually signed with the Red Sox. He made it to Triple A ball (Louisville) before an arm injury ended his career. Interestingly, Niemi signed his name to a Boston Red Sox contract in my house as my father and I looked on.

During my high school baseball career, one game stands out. It was a state tournament game. We trailed, but rallied. I even singled to center field to help fuel the comeback late in the game. However, moments later, I got picked off second base to kill the rally, and we eventually lost. It was another one of those mental funks which managed to trap me from time to time.

I remember the play vividly. I took a lead, started thinking about my girlfriend in the stands, momentarily forgot about the game and got nailed. By the time I reacted, I was out by three or four feet after trying to slide back into second base.

I ran off the field with my head down. My father kicked the dirt and slammed two or three bats on the ground. End of game and beginning of the sullen, silent treatment. Once again, he did not speak to me for weeks. His brooding penetrated my pores, so I avoided him as much as I could.

Another incident quickly comes to mind. It was during batting practice prior to a regular season Middlesex League game. It was my turn to hit with dear old dad pitching. He started off throwing me curve balls. I swung through the first few, missing each pitch and connecting only with air. So what did he do? He continued to throw curve balls, one after another. I whiffed on every one. Frustrated, I took the bat off my shoulder and glared at him. "Throw the damn fastball!" I shouted at him. Then, after he threw another curve, which I foul-tipped, I walked away from the batting screen, cursed, spat and flung the bat away in disgust.

I recall another painful memory. During football practice, I periodically dogged it. And I paid for it, too. After practice, as my teammates headed for the showers, my father forced me to take extra laps around the field. I can still feel the sting after he kicked me in the rear-end and ordered: "Start taking laps around the field and don't stop until I tell you to!"

It was a double punishment. Not only was he disgusted with me, but my teammates also ridiculed me and I lost their respect. "How can you do that?" they used to say. "How can you do that to Coach Carew? He's your father."

There are good memories, too. I had my moments, and many times I played well in both football and baseball. My proudest moment as an athlete, in terms of my relationship with my coach and father, took place when I was a sophomore during practice on a dark and dreary day prior to our football season opener.

Towards the end of practice, the coaches decided to have the squad's first offense scrimmage full-tilt against the scrubs. At the time, I was a linebacker on the scrubs or the reserve squad. I remember feeling especially pumped up. To my mind, the scrimmage turned out to be one of my finest hours.

From my linebacker position, I totally disrupted the first-string varsity offense. I made seven or eight tackles in a row, twice blitzed and smothered ball carriers behind the line of scrimmage, and I even sacked the head coach's son, Bernie Megin, Jr., the first string quarterback.

The better I played, the more my emotions boiled. I even turned defiantly cocky and taunted the team's first string offense. My last tackle was the best. I filled the hole quickly, met a back head-on and stopped the ball-carrier cold with a square, rock-solid hit. Immediately, I jumped up, raised a clenched fist above my head and let out a roar.

By that time, it had started to rain in buckets, and the coaches called off the remainder of the scrimmage. I remember running off the field and I felt someone whack me on the backside. I looked around and saw that the smack on my butt had come from my father. By this time, he and I were running side by side. He was smiling and he shouted, as we ran together, "That's the way to play football. Great job!"

Later that evening, sitting around the family dinner table, my father was still beaming. He shared his satisfaction with the way I had played with the rest of the family: "After the scrimmage, Bernie (head coach Megin) told me: 'Walter, Wally was a tiger out there today. He's only a sophomore, but we have to get him in the starting lineup on defense.' "

That is how I became a sophomore starter on defense, and the memory of that rain-soaked practice is my proudest moment as an athlete.

Back then, sports were not my only interest. Like most boys my age, my hormones were out of control. Girls had become a lot more appealing than sugar and spice and everything nice. Suddenly, pretty, shapely girls were everywhere; three lived next door, and there were three or four more who lived not far away on the same street. Where do you escape? I felt guilty about my feelings. Occasionally, I watched American Bandstand with the forever young Dick Clark as the host. I quickly turned it off if my father came into the room. Only a sissy would watch shows like that, I thought.

How could I talk to him about girls? To begin with, he thought Elvis Presley was vile. I had to talk to someone, so I chose my mother. She stayed at home and ran the house. She cared for everyone and everything—although my father's needs always came first. My father did absolutely nothing around the house. I don't think he ever changed a light bulb.

At the time, I felt strangled by guilt. Dad was both my human father and my spiritual father. I resented that at the time. However, it was from him that I first learned about the wonder and mystery of God, but it was not until years later that I began to appreciate the gift he had given me.

I have great faith today. He planted the seed, something I have never forgotten. In fact, I love the Church and always have, even in the midst of struggles. I remember serving as an altar boy, carrying a freshly washed and pressed white surplice on a hanger and rushing to Our Lady's at 6:30 in the morning. A tremendous priest named Father John Scollan broke me in as an altar boy. While vesting prior to Mass, he kissed each vestment, as a sign of reverence, and carefully explained its liturgical meaning to me.

Father Scollan died with his boots on at the age of seventy-one. On the Saturday afternoon of January 30, 1954, he collapsed and died while hearing confessions.

It just took time for me to truly know and experience God's love. Father Bill Anderson, my longtime, loving spiritual director, and Mary, my wife, were special agents who God used to touch me, draw me close. They gave to me what others, particularly my family, could not—the liberating gift of unconditional love which heals, renews and restores life.

For much of his life, my father went to Mass and communion every day. As kids, the entire family said the rosary after the evening meal during May and October. It was awkward, and all the Carew kids viewed the experience as a dreaded duty. He insisted that I march with him in May processions in honor of the Blessed Mother. I detested marching because none of my friends had to participate. He took me with him when he spent an hour praying before the Blessed Sacrament during 40-hour devotions. He tipped his hat whenever he passed a Catholic church; he ended every day on his knees; he took a rosary to bed; and anytime we went anywhere together, we first had to make a visit to the church. He even went so far as to use sports and coaching as a platform to communicate the Gospel message.

In high school, I not only failed to reach my potential as an athlete, but I was also a poor student. I even flunked out one semester and could not play baseball that spring. I just could not concentrate, no matter how hard I tried. I attended Catholic elementary school and a public high school. I was much happier in Catholic school and did well. Looking back, my parents should have sent me to a Catholic high school, away from my father. But there were six children in my family, and we were trying to get by on a teacher's salary.

I started writing many years ago. I love to write and always have. At some point, I became obsessed with the creative process—turning ideas into sentences, paragraphs and finally stories. I read all I could about writers and still do. I wanted my father to read everything I wrote. If I wrote a piece and he had not read it, I was disappointed. My father was not a writer. It was the only thing I could do better than him.

When my father got sick, my wife and I moved back to my hometown so I could be close to him. I visited him almost every day, kissing him, hugging him and telling him how much I loved him.

At the time, I was a Eucharistic Minister and I was blessed with the opportunity to bring him Holy Communion. It made me feel that the circle was complete; he cooperated with God's grace to give me life, and at the end, I had the honor of bringing the author of all life to him.

He died at age seventy-seven on June 15, 1995, at seven in the morning. Later that day, as I rode an exercise bike, a tune came to my mind. I had not thought of it in years. He often sang it to me when he and I rode in the family car alone. It is called "Bonaventure Brown and White," his college song. Thoughts rushed in and out of my mind. He should not have died on June 15th, I thought. He should have died the day before—June 14th. Flag Day. I kept seeing the color green and I smiled to myself remembering how he always stood just a little bit taller every St. Patrick's Day.

Dad was buried in his American Legion uniform with his coffin turned so that his head faced the American flag (that was his wish). I spoke at his funeral Mass. It was the proudest moment of my life. I felt perfectly confident and in total control, as if I had everyone inside Our Lady's Church in the

Courtesy of the Carew family

The Last Hurrah
Ex-Army Infantry Captain Walter Carew, Sr. marching for the last time—Patriot's Day 1993.

palm of my hand, including Father Pierce, who celebrated the Mass, and the priests on the altar. I walked up the sanctuary steps and bowed before the altar. Without a script, I spoke from my heart for just a few minutes. When I was done, the packed church erupted into applause. I snapped my heels together, saluted my father's casket and returned to my pew. I felt a strange warmth—a glow—despite being so sad. I was numb, but somehow I knew I finally had become my own man.

In the final analysis, what caused both my father and me the most pain is one fact: During his coaching career he helped so many boys. Why couldn't he help me at a time in my life when I needed it most? Why did I block him out? I wish it had been different. To this day, it remains a mystery that I cannot fully explain. For most of my life, I have lived with the feeling that I failed my father. My hardest struggle has been trying to overcome those feelings. To do so, acceptance opened the first crack in the door.

Many times since my father's funeral I have prayed: "Dad, I forgive you for not helping me during the times in my life when I needed you so much. Please forgive me for all the times I disappointed you. I am confident that now you know how much I have always loved you. In your heart, you loved me. I have no doubt about that, even though you found it difficult to express it, to show it."

Cigar Smoke and Sweaty Football Jerseys

T he grandest smells of my youth would be offensive to most people. They were the pungent odor of stale cigar smoke and the reeking scent of dirty, sweat-soaked practice football jerseys piled inside metal lockers.

As a boy, those two smells were sweeter to me than the delicate aroma of a lovely rose.

The period was post-World War II America leading up to and immediately following the Korean War. The years were from 1946 through 1955, midway through the two terms of the Eisenhower Administration. The place was historic Concord, Massachusetts, the high school football capital of the state, New England and the East.

Concord, an old Yankee town of around thirteen thousand, about seventeen miles west of Boston, was the one place in all the land about which spirited songs like "Mr. Touchdown USA" and "You've Got to be a Football Hero to Get Along with the Beautiful Girls" were written. Or so I thought. I was young—turning twelve on December 20, 1955—and at the time, no one could have convinced me otherwise.

The hub of my universe, where Concord High football reigned supreme, was the hallowed, ivy covered Hunt Gymnasium and Emerson Playground. It was there inside a small, brick gymnasium with old-fashioned lanterns on both sides of the entrance and outside on a field of green where mighty Concord teams prepared for and played their home games.

From 1946 through the first three games of the 1952 season, Concord High teams were unbeaten. Only a scoreless tie with arch-rival Lexington on Thanksgiving Day morning in 1947 marred a 58-0-1 record. In fact, through ten seasons, Concord teams lost only three times in the regular season, compiled an 85-3-1 record (not counting two post-season bowl games) and posted eight unbeaten seasons. During that era, Concord split a pair of Piedmont Bowl games in North Carolina, losing 14-13 in 1950; and winning 20-13 in 1951, beating New Hanover High School of Wilmington, North Carolina and future pro football great Sonny Jurgensen.

The architect of that Concord football dynasty was Bernard Edward Megin, the great coach known to everyone as "Bernie." Bernie Megin, the cigar-chomping former third string quarterback at Notre Dame, had a magnetic personality. He was an only child and his family moved to Concord when he was young. His father ran a cleaning business in West Concord. An

Courtesy of the Carew Family

The End of an Era
Concord finished undefeated in 1955, Coach Megin's final unbeaten season and the end of the dynasty. From left: assistant coach John O'Connell, co-captain Jack Hutchinson, Head Coach Bernie Megin, co-captain Andy Horne, and assistant coach Walter Carew, Sr.

all-around athlete, Bernie attracted people like a pied piper. As a coach, he was a pure genius and well ahead of his time.

While in the Navy, he was commissioned an ensign, and he was stationed at the Great Lakes Naval Base in the Midwest, where he crossed paths with many of the greatest football coaches the game has ever known—including Paul Brown (Ohio State, the Cleveland Browns and the Cincinnati Bengals), Jim Tatum (Maryland), Murray Warmath (Minnesota), Bud Wilkinson (Oklahoma), and George Halas (Chicago Bears). Megin was a human sponge around the game's greatest coaches, soaking up every drop of information his brain could hold.

As a coach himself, he ran short, crisp practices. He stressed fundamentals and repetition. His squads ran the same play or drill over and over until it was done right. His teams wore lighter pads and low-cut shoes, accentuating speed and quickness. He had an uncanny eye for talent, shifting a reserve fullback to guard where the player excelled. And he delegated authority, assembling a terrific staff of assistant coaches, then standing back and letting them coach.

One of those assistant coaches was my father, Walter Carew, Sr. He was the backfield coach, a former high school All-Scholastic and a college Hall of Famer at St. Bonaventure University. The line coach was John O'Connell, a burly man with a big heart who grew prize-winning roses. He played baseball at Boston University and, like my father, he also was a legitimate pro baseball prospect. O'Connell was one of the best catching prospects in the area. A handsome man (he actually looks like former Cardinals' catcher turned broadcaster Tim McCarver), O'Connell was a weight-lifter and a physical fitness buff. Also like my father, he never swore, smoked or drank. How tough was O'Connell? As a youth, he developed his defensive skills as a baseball catcher by catching without a mask! Recently, O'Connell told me that many days, after catching without a mask, his eyes were so black and blue that his mother soothed the pain by applying hot olive oil to the sore and disfigured areas.

Ironically, both men hailed from Medford, Massachusetts, where they had been high school teammates in baseball and football, playing for the mighty Mustangs, the old Blue and White. The two grew up one street behind each other and remained close friends until the day my father died.

As the oldest son of an assistant coach, I led a privileged life. I got to shine football shoes, help the players pull their jerseys over shoulder pads and tear tape into strips and hold ankles and knees secure while the body parts were being wrapped by track coach and trainer Harold "Skip" O'Connor—one of my future English teachers. I also patrolled the sidelines, picked the mud out of cleats with tongue depressors, applied a line of greasy, black sun screen under the players' eyes, rubbed Red Hot into a sore back or shoulder and carried a water bucket onto the field during time outs.

Incidentally, O'Connor, a diminutive man—he stood only five feet two inches—was a giant in track and field. His Concord teams, both indoor and outdoor, were state powerhouses. In those days, Concord had more than its share of athletes who were blessed with exceptional speed which benefited not only the school's track and field teams, but the football teams as well.

He grew up in Rhode Island and he was a graduate of Providence College. O'Connor was a celebrated author. He wrote numerous books on track and field. He also worked for the State Department and ran track and field clinics all over the world. Later, he coached track at the College of the Holy Cross, and he is a member of the Holy Cross Sports Hall of Fame. He had a warm personality, a terrific sense of humor (regularly making fun of the fact that he was shorter than Mickey Rooney), and everyone admired him. He fit in perfectly with Coaches Megin, Carew and O'Connell.

It was a charmed life, being the son of an assistant coach, one that made my buddies more than a little bit envious. I even had the opportunity, if I was good, to watch black and white silent football film. Reel after reel. Many nights, my father and I watched football films for hours or until the images on the screen became blurry, and it was time to reluctantly go to bed.

From as far back as I can remember, coaches, athletes, priests, religious, friends, neighbors, and relatives, filed in droves in and out of our house. It was extra-special whenever Coach Megin arrived, day or night. As soon as I spotted him, I spontaneously grabbed a football and jumped over the couch, pretending I was Johnny Lujack, the former All-American Notre Dame quarterback during the late 1940s. More than anything else, I ached just to have him notice me. Whenever he did, even if it was just a pat on the back, I was especially proud that the greatest football coach in the entire world had acknowledged that I—a stumbling, bumbling kid—actually existed; that I lived, breathed and could make eye contact with someone as important as Coach Megin. The biggest bonus of all was that Coach Megin actually liked me.

Megin was about five feet nine inches, and he had put on weight over the years. His physique resembled the Pillsbury Dough Boy, not much different from the way I look today. He was bald, except on the sides. He wore hand-me-down tweed sport jackets, bow ties and a trademark fedora, which more often than not looked like he had sat on it. In contrast, my father was trim, well-built and a sharp dresser; his suits, sports jackets and ties always matched perfectly.

Unlike Megin, my father was a quiet, shy man and deadly serious. Coach Megin taught physical education. My father was an English teacher and a philosopher. He was an expert on Abraham Lincoln, St. Thomas Aquinas and James Joyce.

Coach Megin was never without his ever-present cigar, and his smile was so beguiling that it almost made you dizzy. He was Knute Rockne and Frank Leahy all rolled into one. To me, when he dropped in, it was like having a living legend in our home. The years have gone by alarmingly fast. Every time I smell cigar smoke, I associate the aroma with mild, sweet fra-

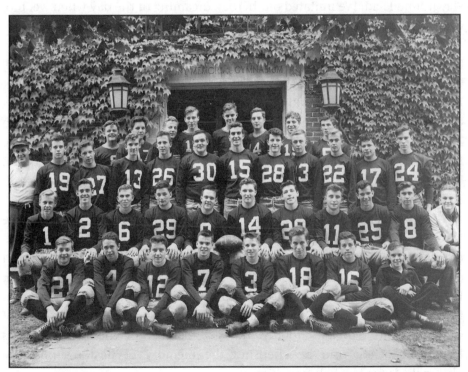

Courtesy of Bruce Woodworth

Undefeated and bowl-bound 1950 Concord High football team.

grances, just because it reminds me of Megin. It gives me a pleasant feeling of well-being, and I don't even smoke cigars.

Concord High's colors are maroon and white, but most of the time Megin's teams wore yellow pants and white jerseys with maroon numbers, two maroon stripes on the sleeves and yellow helmets. Those colors were the trademark of the Concord High football dynasty, although sometimes his teams wore plain maroon jerseys with white numbers, too.

Fall was the most exciting time of the year; autumn meant warm days, cool nights and colorful landscapes, an ideal setting for the game. Football was everything. Football was the only thing. There was no life except for football. High school football. Concord High School football.

Following the home games as darkness settled in, Coach Megin's sons, Bernie Jr., Billy, Neddy and I, threw a football around on the gridiron where mighty Concord High usually had won another game. The stands were empty. Confetti and streamers were strewn on the sacred turf of Emerson Playground Field. We imitated our heroes, dreaming of the day when we, too, would play for Concord High.

What heroes they were, schoolboy football stars who seemed bigger than life! The list of names was endless: Jim McKenna, Leo McKenna, John Pierce, Charlie Hancock, Joe Sweeney, Joe Callahan, Dick Lyons, Bruce Woodworth, Dick Ryan, Bill Hoyt, Jim Ring, Paul McLaughlin, Dave Bouchard, Donnie Cullinane, Jacky King, Tommy Alexander, Ernie Alexander, Lyle Carlson, Bob Zumwalt, Rivers Adams, Charlie Flanigan, Muzzy Muscato, Sal Silvio, Charlie Dee, Jack O'Grady, Dick Loynd, Charlie Bowse, Bobby Davidson, Frank Curran, Jack Hutchinson, Billy Hutchinson, Mike McHugh, Al Dougherty, Ken Olsen and so many others. The names just go on and on.

Two others who stand out were Bob Gray and Mase King. Gray, a place kicker and right-handed pitcher in baseball, was an overachiever whose love of Concord High sports overcame much, both on and off the field. King, an only child, devoted his entire life to his parents. Today, he is a retired teacher. He was educated at Harvard and M.I.T. In high school, he was a reserve out-fielder in baseball and student-manager emeritus during the glory years of Concord High football. Proudly, he is a member of the Boston Braves Historical Society, and he cherishes the memory of Boston's one-time National League baseball franchise.

Both Bernie, Jr. and I did eventually play for Concord High, although at the start of my junior year, they changed the name of the high school, hyphenating it forever by renaming it Concord-Carlisle. I did not like it then, nor do I like it any better today.

Bernie, Jr. and I actually played on the same team. It was 1959, the last season of Concord High football, around the time that Coach Megin outfitted his teams in leather helmets, copying the style worn by Notre Dame at the time. Bernie, Jr. was a senior quarterback and a pure passer, blessed with a strong arm and a velvet-soft touch. I was a sophomore and I was a starter on defense.

Coach Megin, still the head coach, was at the twilight of his career. But Concord was no longer a powerhouse. In fact, we completed that season with a 3-4-2 record.

I played two more seasons for Coach Megin, both the 1960 and 1961 campaigns. We posted a 6-3 record in 1960 and then staggered home with a 2-7 record in 1961. We ended the season losing to a strong Lexington High team, 16-8. It was Coach Megin's final season and his last game as head coach. It also was the last Concord High football game played at Emerson Field, the sight of so much past glory. Beginning the next season, the fall of 1962, the school played its varsity football games at a field located on the grounds of the new high school which had opened in 1960.

Interestingly, the Boston Patriots and the old American Football League debuted in 1960. Thanks to Coach Megin and postmaster Ed McCaffery, who was a friend of Billy Sullivan, the Patriots' owner, the pro football team practiced in Concord at Emerson Field during its inaugural season.

During the fall of 1960, the Boston Patriots and the Concord High Patriots practiced on the same field. The Concord Armory served as a base for the first-year AFL team. Before the season was over, just about every youth in Concord, including me, was seen walking around town in a Boston Patriots practice jersey. Later, I wound up working for the Patriots, as the assistant public relations director in 1971, the year that Foxboro Stadium was built and Quarterback Jim Plunkett arrived from Stanford.

Prior to his final season, Coach Megin had been ill for some time and he died just a few years later on March 24, 1964. He was only 49. At the time, I was in the Army and stationed in Germany. Sadly, Bernie Megin, Jr. died soon after his father. Like his father, he had a charismatic personality. Also like his father, he died of the same illness, an implacable disease that attacks the entire human being. Both deaths were tragedies.

And so those memories of a golden Concord High football era, which made for a special boyhood, are tinged with sadness. For most boys growing up in Concord, Concord High football was the only game in town and the source of thrills and fantasies. But the other boys' fathers were not coaches. More importantly, their fathers were not our football coaches. But Bernie's father and my father were. And that was part of our joy and, to some extent, part of our sorrow.

The Football Priests

During its fifty-nine game unbeaten football streak which lasted from 1946-52, Concord High School, a public school, graduated many student-athletes who achieved success in a number of fields. It also produced two future priests, the late Father Charles B. Hancock, S.J. and Father John Joseph "Chipper" Pierce, O.F.M.

In high school, both were outstanding all-around athletes. Father Pierce also played college football. He starred for St. Bonaventure University and St. Michael's College in Vermont, where he and his high school and college teammate, Jim McKenna, transferred after the Bonnies dropped football.

The faith transmitted through their loving families was instrumental in each man's decision to pursue a religious vocation. Competitive athletics, and football in particular, helped cultivate the seeds of spirituality. Through the ups and downs of the sport, the riveting loyalty of teammates, the drive to excel, the importance of self-sacrifice, plus the opportunity to grasp a glimmer of the redemptive potential of pain, Fathers Hancock and Pierce both learned, at an early age, values that are everlasting.

During their high school football careers, both young athletes experienced severe injuries. As a senior in 1952, the year that Concord High's unbeaten streak finally ended, Hancock broke a leg in the opening game. He never played another down. He had scored a touchdown in the 19-0 victory, but his football career had ended prematurely and painfully.

Pierce was also a senior when he was injured in 1949. He blew out a knee in the sixth game of the season, another 19-0 Concord victory. Like Hancock, he, too, scored a touchdown earlier in the game. His team finished the year with a 10-0-0 record, but Pierce watched the last four games from the sidelines.

Both athletes turned adversity into an opportunity to examine their priorities: who they were as people and what direction their lives should take. For years, all the Catholics on Concord football teams attended, with the coaches and even some Protestant teammates, a Saturday morning Mass on the day of the game. It was part of the pre-game ritual, as important as the pre-game meal and the pre-game taping.

Football players spend much quiet time preparing for the opening kick-off. The quiet time at Mass and the hush in the pre-game locker room established the mood: athletes readying themselves for a battle, one that would demand a total commitment and force each of them to willingly place their bodies in harm's way. Many a football player has experienced nausea and has actually thrown up awaiting the game's first collision.

I know I did on a couple of occasions.

Quiet time is especially conducive to prayer. Both Pierce and Hancock prayed during the years they played football, and the seeds of their religious vocations could have taken root during those special times of solitude.

Following his own injury, Pierce experienced darkness in his life, but

Courtesy of Dana Pierce

Pierce playing for St. Michael's College.

his parents, Ralph and Frances, refused to let him feel sorry for himself. "We want you to hold your head high, stand up and be a man," they told him. So for the first time, he began to consider life beyond football. "I think it was the first time it crossed my mind that God might have something else besides sports and football in store for me," he said.

As a Concord High Hall of Famer, Pierce never tasted defeat during his schoolboy football career. In college, he and teammate McKenna, also a Concord High Hall of Famer, played for coach Joe Bach at St. Bonaventure. Bach was one of the Seven Mules at Notre Dame—the linemen who blocked for that still famous backfield "The Four Horsemen." Pierce was such a good athlete that years later, at age forty-one, he played varsity hockey at Fairleigh Dickinson University, where he enrolled in music courses.

After college, Pierce spent two years in the Army before entering the seminary where he joined the Franciscan order and studied for the priesthood. He was ordained on March 2, 1963 in Washington, D.C. While serving as a priest in the order founded by St. Francis of Assisi in the 13th Century, Father Pierce says he has experienced suffering as well as great joy, especially while ministering to the elderly, the sick and the dying.

Early in his priesthood, Father Pierce served as a Catholic chaplain in Vietnam. He was a Captain with the 1st United States Marine Division in Chu-Lai, about twenty-five miles southwest of DaNang.

It was an unforgettable experience. "Hell on earth," he calls it.

Most of the fighting was done at night. The exhausted Marines tried to get what little rest they could during the day. Fires burned constantly from the barrage of small weapons and artillery fire. Many of the Marines picked up jungle rot and it took weeks for the painful sores to heal. Skirmishes with the enemy could erupt at any moment, and they often took place less than one thousands yards away.

"Sometimes the Marines were so tired that they couldn't even carry the mail bags. I had to reach over and lift them off their shoulders," Father Pierce recalls.

Father Pierce was awarded the Bronze Star for valor. He worked with the medical evacuation teams as they rushed wounded and dying Marines into waiting helicopters.

Courtesy of the Carew family

Father Pierce celebrating Mass in Vietnam.

What he remembers most about the year he spent in Vietnam is the courage of individuals. "Their faithfulness to duty stands out in my mind. The conditions were horrendous, but the Marines were there to serve their country by fighting the war. It was a privilege and an honor to serve them," he said.

Like Pierce, Hancock was a gifted athlete. In football, Charlie was a swift, shifty back. "He was tough to bring down," said ex-teammate Ken Olsen, the Golden Boy of Concord sports and also a Hall of Famer. "But what I remember most about Charlie is that he was a terrific person."

He was class treasurer in 1953, a member of the National Honor Society, a Good Citizenship Award winner, a member of the senior class executive committee and his classmates voted him "the most respected male in the graduating class."

His nickname was "Diz." Charlie never swore. If he was upset, he would say "that dizzy such and such or so and so." He said it so often that all his friends started calling him "Diz".

Throughout high school, Charlie was a regular guy. He hung around with a terrific bunch of young men. He dated regularly and he enjoyed having a good time. After attending Boston College for a year and studying the spiritual teachings of St. Ignatius Loyola, the founder of the Jesuits, he decided to enter the Order.

Charlie was a quiet person and his announcement caught everyone by surprise. He picked Emerson Playground to share the news with one of his closest friends, Joe Sweeney, another capable Concord athlete.

"It was after a softball game," said Sweeney, "when Charlie told me he intended to study for the priesthood and that he wanted to become a Jesuit."

Hancock entered the Society of Jesus on July 30, 1954. His brother Jim drove him to Shadow Brook in Lenox, Massachusetts. But the trip through the beautiful Berkshires was anything but serene.

"I got stopped for speeding," remembered Jim Hancock. "The state trooper even made us open up a trunk we had in the back and empty out all of Charlie's belongings."

Father Charlie Hancock was a Jesuit for thirty-nine years. He was ordained a priest on June 8, 1968. He held four masters degrees, one in philosophy, a second in theology, a third in sociology and a fourth in linguistics. "That has to be some kind of record," said Father Joseph R. Fahey, S.J., the president of Boston College High School and a close personal friend. "If it is not, I pity the person who holds the record."

Father Hancock spent much of his priesthood as a missionary in Japan, teaching at Sophia University in Tokyo and working with the poor. In fact, he moved into an apartment in a working class neighborhood and opened a coffee shop. To get to class, he drove a motor bike back and forth to the University.

Father Charlie Hancock died of cancer on March 14, 1993. He was fifty-eight years old. Shortly before he died, he returned to Japan. It was a painful decision, leaving family and friends knowing he would never see them again. Love is never an easy decision. At his funeral Mass in Tokyo, Christians and non-Christians packed the church. Father Hancock was buried in a plain, white coffin. Before he was buried, his Japanese students and friends circled his coffin and spoke out loud, telling him how much they loved him and thanking him for bringing the light of Christ into their lives.

Later, at a memorial Mass for Father Hancock, Father Fahey eulogized his friend and fellow Jesuit. He concluded his remarks by saying: "Thank you, Charlie, for showing all of us what it means to be a priest and what it means to be a Jesuit."

A loving family, rich friendships and unforgettable teammates, sharing the joys of playing sports, especially the great game of football, helped nurture Charlie as his vision of a better world took shape and he served God and his fellow men and women.

At a memorial Mass for her uncle, Father Hancock's niece, Ellen Blake, spoke for the entire Hancock family when she said: "He touched all of us deeply, and he will always live in our hearts."

How much of a role did football play in shaping these two men? It is impossible to say. But it seems obvious that many of the qualities they displayed in playing football, qualities such as courage and commitment, came into play as they served as priests.

Courtesy of Dana Pierce

Fathers Hancock and Pierce.

1953 Concord High School Bat Boys
Bernie Megin, Jr. and Wally Carew, Jr.

The Two Luckiest Boys in the Whole Wide World

For one glorious day in June 1953, a pair of precocious Concord teenagers knocked the Boston Red Sox battery of pitcher Mel Parnell and catcher Sammy White off center stage at Fenway Park.

Their names are Dave Bouchard, also known as "Boo," and Dave DiRuzzo, who was nicknamed "Porky." On that sweetest of June days in 1953, Bouchard and DiRuzzo led Concord to a nail-biting 5-4 victory over Somerville in the semi-finals of the old Class A Eastern Massachusetts Baseball Tournament at the Taj Mahal of baseball in New England, Fenway Park.

At the time, Manager Lou Boudreau's Red Sox were on the road. Boston finished fourth that year behind—who else?—Casey Stengel's New York Yankees. Mickey Vernon of the Senators won the American League batting title (.337). Cleveland Indians' third baseman and slugger Al Rosen won the home run (43) and RBI (145) titles. Harry Agganis tore up the International League (.288, 22 homers, 104 RBIs) playing for the Louisville Colonels. Two years later, Agganis, the promising Red Sox first baseman, would be dead at age twenty-six.

But in early June 1953, summer was fast approaching, the schoolboys had taken over Fenway Park and life was filled with wondrous possibilities.

47

I know because I was there. I was one of two Concord bat boys. The other was Bernie Megin, Jr., son of Concord football coach, Bernie Megin, Sr. My father was the Concord baseball coach. I was nine, Bernie, Jr. was eleven, and for a few unforgettable days we were the two luckiest boys in the world.

Bouchard, a stylish southpaw, who was so skinny his Adam's apple stuck out, pitched eight-plus strong innings. DiRuzzo, a barrel-chested catcher, clouted a three-run home run, a tremendous shot over the Green Monster (left field wall) and high into the screen above the 379-foot mark, just to the left of the flag pole.

In the ninth, Concord's ace, right-hander Alan Stockellburg, who later pitched in the Milwaukee Braves' minor league chain, relieved Bouchard with the bases loaded and preserved the win by striking out the only two hitters he faced.

In the finals the next day, also at Fenway Park, Concord lost to Milford and its strong-armed southpaw, Ralph Lumenti, 3-1. Later, Lumenti made it

Courtesy of Dave Bouchard

Fantasy at Fenway
Concord High's pitcher Dave Bouchard and catcher Dave DiRuzzo walk off the field during the Class A Eastern Massachusetts Tournament.

to The Show and he pitched briefly for the Washington Senators and managers Chuck Dressen and Cookie Lavagetto.

However, the biggest winners were young Bernie and me. With eyes as wide as watermelons, we saw everything, missed nothing. Being on the field, sitting in the dugouts, running in the outfield. Touching the left-field wall. Drinking out of a big league water fountain. For baseball-crazy kids, it was like dying and going to heaven.

My brother, Tommy also was at Fenway. He was only six, and he had to sit in the stands, although he got loose and wandered all over the ball park. He even bumped into Curt Gowdy, the Red Sox TV broadcaster.

"Hi, Red," Gowdy said to my reddish-blond haired brother.

Tommy came home with a couple of baseballs, but he got the biggest kick out of the fact that Curt Gowdy called him "Red." He talked about it for weeks and even mentioned it years later.

DiRuzzo, the home run-hitting catcher, has lived in the South for years, and he currently resides in Brandon, Florida. Today, he clearly remembers the pitch he clouted for a home run at Fenway Park.

"It was a high, hard one," he said, speaking from his home in Florida. "I didn't know it was gone, that I had hit a home run, until I reached second base and saw the umpire giving the signal."

At the time, the burly Concord catcher felt like pinching himself. "My first thought was that I was dreaming," he said. "But then I said to myself: 'Dear Lord, if this is a dream, I never want to wake up!' It took awhile for it to sink in that I had hit a home run at *Fenway Park*."

After high school, DiRuzzo headed to the University of Florida on a football scholarship, and the commotion over his home run at Fenway followed him. "Once the Florida press found out about the home run, all they wanted to talk and write about was the home run that this high school kid from up north hit at Fenway Park," he said.

Later, DiRuzzo earned a Ph.D. and he spent his career in education, serving as superintendent of schools in Louisville, Kentucky, New Orleans, Louisiana, Starkville, Mississippi, and Fort Pierce, Florida. Today, he is back doing what he loves best—teaching. "I am easing into retirement by returning to my first love," he said. "And that is teaching in the classroom."

DiRuzzo and Bouchard were a brainy baseball battery. Both became educators. Bouchard played football and baseball at Brandeis University. Later, he taught mathematics at his high school alma mater.

As an athlete, Bouchard was a natural, as smooth as silk. He married young and quickly had to support a family. After college, he rejected an offer to play professional baseball. "The Cleveland Indians offered me $5,000 without a tryout," he recalled. "To get more money, I would have had to go to Cleveland for a tryout. But I had a teaching job lined up, so I decided to take it."

In high school, Bouchard, who was a clever quarterback in football, pitched many memorable games. They included a 3-2 extra-inning victory over arch-rival Lexington and its hard-throwing right-hander Don Nottebart. Nottebart later pitched nine seasons in the big leagues (3.65 ERA and 36 wins) for the Houston Colt 45s, Braves, Reds, Yankees and Cubs.

There were two more players on that Concord High team with big-league baseball potential. One was Kenny Olsen and the other was Dick Ballou. Olsen, a blond flash, was a shortstop, had all the tools, and was a terrific all-around athlete. A breakaway halfback in football, he could hit with power, run, field, and throw. The New York Yankees were interested in him and invited Olsen to a tryout in Springfield, Massachusetts.

Believe it or not, Olsen refused to go. "I was just a country bumpkin," said Olsen, remembering the golden days of his youth. "As far as I was concerned, Springfield was on the other side of the earth."

So instead of playing professional baseball, Olsen settled for a long and successful career as a real estate salesman in his hometown which he never left.

Ballou, a freshman, was a utility infielder on the 1953 team. After graduating from high school, he played professional baseball in the Washington Senators' minor league system before turning to sales and coaching.

In the championship game, an outfield error and a mental lapse on the base paths doomed Concord. My father's team loaded the bases with two outs in the ninth, but a strike out ended the game. Too bad, because the team's best hitter, Olsen, was on-deck waiting to hit.

Following losses, my father usually was the last one out of the locker room. He took defeat hard. Sometimes he did not get home until after the rest of the family had eaten. My mother was an expert at keeping his supper warm in the oven without spoiling it.

However, after losing the championship game at Fenway Park, there was no lingering at the ballpark. Shortly after the final out, the bus was loaded and headed back to Concord. It was a silent ride home, much different than the previous day, following the 5-4 victory over Somerville. After the thrilling win, Mrs. Betty Mattison, Concord dairy farm owner and mother of first baseman Jack Mattison, instructed the bus driver to stop at Howard Johnson's where she bought everyone jumbo banana splits.

I ate too much ice cream and became sick. The combination of ice cream and the excitement of an experience of a lifetime was too much for a nine-year-old's stomach to take. When we got home, I skipped the meat loaf and mashed potatoes and went straight to bed.

With an ache in my belly and a head full of dreams.

Eddie

Eddie Dalton
Concord High School, Class of 1961

A Special Teammate

During the fall of 1960, he and I were football teammates. He was a year ahead of me in high school. I remember feeling admiration mixed with envy when I learned that he would continue his education at the University of Notre Dame.

We went our separate ways. After that, our paths may have crossed two or three more times at most.

Life moved along. Then one day the numbing news came. It spread by word of mouth. It was mid-afternoon. The sky was bright blue and the summer sun sparkled. I was angry and I wished it was raining.

Today, Edward J. Dalton, Jr. is but one of the fifty-eight thousand names that are inscribed on the Vietnam Memorial in Washington, D.C. He died fighting for his country, in an unpopular war, far away from home.

U.S. Army 2nd Lieutenant Dalton died on Sunday, August 14, 1966. That morning, he participated in a Mass on the battlefield and received the Eucharist before leading his infantry unit on a patrol. He was killed as he was riding in a jeep when his squad was ambushed.

For both Eddie and me, home was Concord—the quaint, historic Massachusetts town where other soldiers—Patriots—fired the first shots of the Revolutionary War. He and I had much in common. We both were Irish

Catholic and had been students at a parochial elementary school named after a local convert, Rose Hawthorne.

We were also altar boys, crossing guards, and veterans of a rough-and-tumble recess game called Keep-Away. At least once a week, the Sisters of the Holy Union would call a halt to the game after they spotted the first bloody nose which, more often than not, left a dark red stain on a starched white shirt.

Later on, Eddie became an honor role student at Concord High School. He was a neat dresser, an accomplished dancer who made every female partner think she was Ginger Rogers, and a substitute end on the varsity football team.

In fact, he was a better dancer than a football player. Eddie wore number 83—a maroon number on a white jersey trimmed in maroon and gold. He was designated an end by Coach Bernie Megin primarily because of his height. He was over six feet tall, and the coaches grouped him with all the prospects who were not gifted enough to play in the backfield or burly enough to man the line.

For Eddie, the joy of football was being a member of the team—us against them, our town, our school, and our colors versus their town, their school and their colors. He loved the identity, the camaraderie and the esprit de corps, individuals making personal sacrifices for a common good and common goal. It was that special bond that Eddie loved most about the great game.

Eddie was loyal. The team always came first. He never missed a practice. While others, including me, straggled out of the locker room, he was the first player on the practice field. The early arrivals carried the equipment. He always was honored to carry a bag of footballs or push a blocking sled into the proper position. He led the pack during the pre-practice lap around the field and no one exerted himself more during calisthenics and sprints. Eddie never "dogged" it, and every member of the team respected him.

I never knew until years later, after speaking with his mother, that Eddie contracted polio when he was a child. Years of special exercises helped him strengthen his legs and eventually live a normal life, which for him included playing football and later completing rugged Army infantry training.

Eddie was a wholesome guy. He never swore or participated in any off-color conversation. He was a very moral person, a quiet leader who wore button-down shirts under a maroon Concord jacket and had his black hair clipped short. Back then, the haircut was called a "flat-top." He was polite and reserved, except on the dance floor. He might have been the only boy in the entire school who you would be proud to have date your sister.

His family looked up to him just as much as everyone else. "I was in awe of him," said his younger sister, Kathleen, who grew up to become a wife, mother and teacher at St. Christopher's Catholic School in Nashua, New Hampshire. "It was unfair, hard to live up to. But I always looked to him to do the right thing. You could count on Eddie."

In delicate adolescent social decisions, Kathleen sought her older brother's approval, even when it came to the clothes she wore on a date. "I wanted him to check out what I was wearing and to tell me if I looked OK," she said.

During high school, Eddie worked hard to prepare himself for college. "During Lent, he went to Mass and received Communion every day," said his mother, Marguerite. "He prayed hard that he would get into college."

Justifiably, Eddie was especially proud in the spring of 1965 when he graduated from the University of Notre Dame with a Bachelor of Science Degree in business. "He loved Notre Dame," said his mother. "He was involved in so many activities. Eddie loved every second he spent there."

A big part of Eddie will never leave Notre Dame. During a visit to Notre Dame for the 1998 ND-Stanford football game, my wife, Mary, and I explored the handsome Pasquerilla ROTC Center. Inside the Army Leadership Lounge, I felt that Eddie was present; I could sense his spirit.

Today, his home town honors his memory in a special way. Attached to the "Dalton Road" sign in Concord is a plaque that reads: "Edward J. Dalton, Jr. Born June 10, 1943. Killed in action in Vietnam on August 14, 1966."

As a youth, many predicted that one day he would study for the priesthood. Monsignor John York, the late pastor of St. Bernard's Parish in Concord, often told Mrs. Dalton, "I always thought that your boy would become a priest."

He was never ordained, but his life was marked by faithfulness and service to others. Shortly before Eddie shipped out to Vietnam, his parents visited him while he was stationed at Fort Carson, Colorado. "He had a lot of older men under him," said his mother, recalling the visit. "And many of them told his father and me how good Eddie was to them."

Eddie volunteered for a tour of duty in Vietnam. "He was convinced he could handle it," his mother said. "He told us, 'I'm better trained than those kids who are getting killed over there.' "

The years have flown by, but I have never forgotten my former team-mate, Eddie Dalton, old number 83.

Far more important, however, I pray that he hasn't forgotten me. "I know, Eddie, that the work of intercession is big business in heaven. But would you intercede for me now and then? Please remember me, your ex-high school football teammate. Oh, by the way, in case you forgot, I wore number 60."

Eddie is buried at St. Bernard's cemetery in Concord, about fifty yards from where my father was laid to rest on June 19, 1995.

A Tiger Named McKenna

Fearless men and women, many would say, are not people who have never been afraid. Quite the contrary, they are people who look fear squarely in the eye, and they may blink or flinch, but they push forward.

I have met a few fearless people and read and heard stories about others. But when it comes to fearlessness, I never met anyone who could match James Richard McKenna.

Many years ago, McKenna coached high school football. It was the day before Thanksgiving and the traditional Turkey Day football game, so popular in Massachusetts. Driving by a pond on the way to practice, he noticed a woman standing in water up to her waist frantically reaching for a bobbing object. Obviously, she was not taking a recreational dip in the chilly November waters of New England.

The "object" was the woman's four year old son, who was floating face down in the water. Fortunately, the child wore a snow suit, which made the boy buoyant and probably saved the child's life.

In a flash, McKenna braked his car, pushed open the side door, rushed to the shore and plunged into the water. After pulling the youngster out of the water and laying him on the safety of land, McKenna applied mouth-to-mouth resuscitation for forty minutes, until EMT help arrived and whisked the boy to a nearby hospital. His heroics saved the boy's life. For his efforts, the American Red Cross awarded McKenna a citation and a gold medal.

Unfortunately for Jim, he never made it to football practice that day. "I was physically and emotionally wiped out," said McKenna, remembering the incident.

Even without its head coach, his team won its big game the following day, so justice prevailed. Or maybe an angel stood in for McKenna and guided his team through its final preparations for the biggest game of the season.

Angels have guarded Jim McKenna his entire life. And he has made them work, too, because few have been tested and have responded to all challenges with as much gusto as he has during the course of his life.

As a child, Jim's home life was a far cry from "Ozzie and Harriet" or "Leave It To Beaver." It was hardly ideal and his life was filled with difficulty and pain. Not only was he a troubled youth, but he was also blind-sided by the post World War II epidemic known as polio.

When he was fifteen, McKenna became ill around August of his sophomore year in high school. It was 1947. When school started, he missed both class time as well as important football practices. Despite his weakened condition—he was down to 130 pounds—he was scheduled to start for his team in its opening football game of the season. However, instead of playing, he was rushed to a local hospital where Dr. Charles Dustin diagnosed the illness as polio and immediately had McKenna transferred to Massachusetts General Hospital.

What followed were months of quarantine during which doctors and nurses were his only visitors. The disease wracked his body and the constant isolation withered his spirit. "I was confined to a single room in an iron lung they kept turning on and off," remembered McKenna. "I believed the world had come to an end and my life was over. It seemed like all hell was breaking loose and in my head I was screaming for relief. No one told me anything, except that I had this dreaded thing called polio and that there was something terribly wrong with me. My greatest fear was not knowing what was ahead."

Slowly, however, McKenna recovered. From December 1947, when he was discharged from the hospital, until May 1948, Jim underwent grueling rehabilitation, seven days each week at Mass General. Both knees were locked in braces that extended to his ankles. His right arm was immobilized by a cumbersome support, and he could not walk without the aid of crutches.

Miraculously, in the spring of 1948, McKenna boldly showed up at high school baseball practice. When the team spotted him hobbling on crutches, the players applauded. Jim badgered his coach, my father, until he finally allowed McKenna to take a few swings with a bat. With great joy, he leaned his crutches against the bleachers and reached down to grab a bat. The next thing he remembered he was lying flat on his back and gazing at a hospital ceiling once again.

Just as McKenna was about to select at bat, a bat slipped out of the hands of another player, who was taking a practice swing, and smashed or whipped it across Jim's face and mouth. With frightening force, the flying bat fractured his jaw, broke his nose, grotesquely repositioning it on his face, and knocked out fifteen teeth.

However, by this time, McKenna had been totally transformed. His troubled home life and the battle with polio had toughened him. He had known physical pain, emotional agony and spiritual despair, and he had risen above it all. Nothing could possible crush him in the future. Now, he possessed an iron will.

Coach Carew, became his personal mentor, his champion, his adopted father. My father loved McKenna totally and unconditionally. It was easier for him to love McKenna than it was for him to show the same kind of affection to his own sons and daughters, including me. I will never truly understand it. Nor do I have to. I have long since stopped asking why. I have accepted it. My father was every bit as human as anyone else, even though many, including me, attempted to put him on a pedestal.

"He saved my life," said McKenna. "I was ready to quit, to give up. I needed to know that someone really cared about me. Walter Carew gave me the one thing I needed most, his heart. And because of him, I found hope where before I had none."

From that point on Jim McKenna became a tiger, and nothing and no one would ever conquer him again. From the pit and anguish of nihilism, he had begun to experience spiritual exultation—"soaring on mighty eagles' wings."

By the time the 1948 football season rolled around, all setbacks were in the past and McKenna became a star on an undefeated Concord High football team. As a senior, he wore the unlucky number "13," was voted the team's most valuable player, and helped lead Coach Bernie Megin's team, one of the finest in the school's history, to a perfect 10-0 record. For his efforts, he was enshrined as a charter member of the Concord High Athletic Hall of Fame.

In all sports, McKenna was a brawler. After one football game which he won on a slashing run late in the contest, he admittedly started a melee that had to be calmed by a peace conference at the 50-yard line involving coaches, officials, players and even police.

Another time, in baseball, an opposing player from Winchester, tagged a sliding McKenna just a bit too hard. Immediately, McKenna challenged the opposing infielder, who took one look at the fire in McKenna's bulging eyes and fled. McKenna chased him off the field. When last seen, the Winchester infielder was still running with his tail between his legs looking for a place to hide. Today, McKenna is the first to say that there is no place for fighting in sports. The stories simply illustrate the type of rage that motivated him. When it came to intensity, no one stored more fire than Jim McKenna.

McKenna and two of his high school teammates, Father John Pierce, O.F.M. and the late Joe Callahan, who are also Concord High Hall of Famers, attended St. Bonaventure University on football scholarships.

Courtesy of Dana Pierce

Pure Blood and Guts

There was nothing flashy about the way McKenna played football.

In college, McKenna suffered another setback. He broke a leg. However, once he recovered, he became a starter and played every down for the Bonnies at halfback and linebacker. One of McKenna's most memorable college football victories was a thrilling 22-21 win over the University of Louisville and the Cardinals' star quarterback, future NFL Hall of Famer Johnny Unitas.

Seven of McKenna's college teammates, including Ted Marchiabroda (quarterback) and Jack Butler (halfback), played in the National Football League. Both Marchiabroda—the former head coach of the Baltimore Ravens—and Butler played for the Pittsburgh Steelers. Butler was an all-pro defensive back with Pittsburgh.

Father Pierce tells a story about how hard McKenna and Butler tangled one day during one-on-one drills. "Butler was Coach Joe Bach's favorite," said Father Pierce, laughing as he spoke. "McKenna just ate him up. He knocked Butler down and climbed all over him. We had to pull Jim off of Butler. Jim had that rare gift of fire on the football field. He could let it all out."

During his career as a coach and educator, McKenna coached football at several high schools, and he was elected to the State Football Coaches Hall of Fame.

Courtesy of Dana Pierce

Teammates Pierce and McKenna

McKenna holds three master's degrees, two in education and one in economics. He is a military veteran and served in the Intelligence branch of the U.S. Army. He has a pilot's license, and for years he ran a successful European Ski Trip Business. Business-wise, everything he touched turned to gold.

Before he retired, he served as the director of the Archdiocese of Boston's Alpha-Omega House, a last-chance rehabilitation program for emotionally and behaviorally impaired, criminally involved, high risk boys between the ages of 14-17. "I loved the work," said McKenna. "It was an opportunity to give back some of what I have received to others."

Jim and his wife, Martha, who also was an educator, raised eight children. Sports rescued Jim McKenna. Through athletics, especially football, he received the love that enabled his belief in himself to grow, his faith in God to blossom, and to develop his own potential in many areas and numerous fields.

In the final analysis, McKenna is a human tiger. Compared to him, other so-called tough guys are merely kittens.

Jerry Minihan
Center for the Georgetown University Hoyas

The Bishop Was a Lineman

When Jeremiah Francis Minihan excelled both as an over-achieving high school and college athlete, it was only a foretaste of things to come.

As a collegian, Minihan was an undersized center on Coach Lou Little's gritty Georgetown University football team during the golden era known as the 1930s. Little later coached Columbia and led the Lions to a shocking upset of powerhouse Army in 1947.

When he first spotted Minihan, Little was certain "the little Irishman with a twinkle in his eyes" had a better chance of becoming a cheerleader than he did anchoring the Georgetown line. But that was before the Haverhill, Massachusetts native earned his legendary coach's respect and praise. "Jerry Minihan was the greatest one hundred fifty pound college football center that has ever lived," said Little, reflecting on Bishop Minihan's college football career.

Because of his size, Minihan appeared over-matched in the middle of the line. However, what he lacked in bulk, he more than compensated for with quickness and toughness.

Years later, when Coach Little, a college football Hall of Famer, heard the news that his former player had been named a bishop, he exclaimed, "I have never coached a finer man. My prayers have indeed been answered!"

A game between Georgetown and Pennsylvania epitomized Minihan's competitiveness throughout his athletic career. Penn was Coach Little's alma mater and was heavily favored as the rivals prepared to battle at Philadelphia's historic Franklin Field. One of the Quaker's stars was a burly All-American center named Ed Thompson, who weighed well over two hundred pounds.

Penn won a ferocious defensive battle 3-0 on a field goal late in the game. The two teams waged a holy war, especially in the trenches where Minihan and Thompson hit so hard each man cracked his shoulder pads. In fact, the countless collisions left both linemen completely exhausted, so much that both Minihan and Thompson had to be carried off the field. As the rival linemen were carted away, the large Franklin Field crowd stood and applauded their gallantry.

Minihan's friend and teammate Jack Hagerty, who later coached the Hoyas and served as Georgetown's athletic director, recalled at the time of Minihan's elevation to the episcopacy the toll that Penn game had taken on the future bishop. "Jerry took a frightful amount of punishment," said Hagerty, remembering the bruising battle. "He was the most battered and beaten football player I had ever seen. But he radiated joy, because although we lost, everyone knew that Georgetown had won a moral victory."

Defeat in athletics is a little like death. Perhaps a chunk of Minihan died on the gridiron that fall afternoon in Philadelphia. But by giving his all for the Blue and Gray of Georgetown, the future bishop won a share of glory. His selfless effort transcended the loss.

As he did with football, Jeremiah Minihan brought a fiery zeal to the office of bishop. The Church was his deepest love and the center of his life until the day he died—August 14, 1973—while on vacation in Dublin, Ireland.

Father Gilbert S. Phinn, the pastor at St. Elizabeth's Parish in Milton, Massachusetts, was Bishop Minihan's secretary for several years. Father Phinn still exudes filial love for a man who was both his mentor and his model. He also vested the bishop's body following his death, after it was returned to the United States from Ireland.

"He was a manly guy, but a priest through and through," recalled Father Phinn. "He had a great sense of humor and was a marvelous story teller. But he was always a *Churchman*, not just a churchman. There is a big difference, you know. He had the same mind as the Church in all things—not a day later, or a day sooner, but when the Church says so!"

At one time, Bishop Minihan served as secretary to William Cardinal O'Connell. Later he was chancellor of the Archdiocese of Boston under Richard Cardinal Cushing. Father Phinn, who still refers to the late bishop as "The Boss," recalled that Bishop Minihan also was a skilled diplomat.

"He was a buffer between an old Cardinal and the much younger priests," said Father Phinn. "His door was always open. When priests wanted the ear of the Cardinal, but their timing was inappropriate, he would tell them: 'Not today, I'll call you when the time is right.' The priests could not be convinced that he did not have a hand in every key appointment."

Courtesy of the Archdiocese of Boston

Bishop Jeremiah Minihan (on right) with Boston's Richard Cardinal Cushing

Typical of the bishop, he was a hands-on clergyman. Father Phinn related that, when the bishop was a pastor, he often pulled on his Georgetown sweater and got behind the wheel of a snow plow. Father Phinn also experienced, first hand, brisk two-hour walks all over the Eternal City when he and Bishop Minihan were in Rome for the Second Vatican Council. "That man could walk all afternoon," said Father Phinn, remembering that he had to push himself just to keep up with the bishop.

Most of all, Father Phinn still marvels at the bishop's marvelous mixture of strength and gentleness. "He was most vigorous in his priesthood, but at the same time gentle and kind with people," said Father Phinn. "In a pastoral sense, he was a shepherd and in a biblical sense he was present for others, always caring, watchful and willing to sacrifice."

Bishop Minihan, who studied at the North American College in Rome, was fluent in Italian. He could go into the North End of Boston, known for its Italian heritage and speak to people in their native tongue. Once, he used his familiarity with the language to console a brother Georgetown athlete.

The occasion was one of the greatest college football games ever played, or so declared the late, great father of modern sports writing, Grantland Rice. The year was 1940 and the game pitted Georgetown against Boston College, a battle between two Jesuit Catholic universities and football powerhouses. It was played at Fenway Park.

Boston College prevailed, 19-18, only after quarterback and punter Charlie O'Rourke retreated into his own end zone as the game clock wound down in the fourth quarter and took a safety to preserve the victory. Following the game, the future bishop was seen in the Georgetown locker room with his arm around Augie Lio speaking softly in Italian to the All-American Hoyas' guard.

Minihan was consecrated a bishop on September 8, 1954, which happened to be a special Marian Year. On September 8th, many years previously, he drove his sister, Sister Jeremiah Minihan, SSJ, to the novitiate on the day she entered the convent. And, as a boy, his mother fed him a steady diet of devotion to the Blessed Mother, whose birthday the Church celebrates on September 8th.

Minihan's first official act as a bishop was to walk over to his eighty-four year old father, Timothy—the patriarch of the Haverhill, Massachusetts family—kiss him on the cheek and bless him. Weeks later, when he was named an Honorary Doctor of Humane Letters by his alma mater,

Georgetown, Bishop Minihan showed his reverence for true authority when he said: "Universal jurisdiction over the life of man lies only within the providence of God. Reduce that to world power and to world domination of the state, over the material and spiritual elements of human life, and mankind will be robbed of the end and purpose of his being and the eternal reward of his earthly existence!"

Bishop Minihan championed the Church through devoted service to the people of God. He believed that obedience opened the door to holiness, obedience to his parents, the Cardinal Archbishops under whom he served, and the Pope—all of whom he saw as human channels pouring forth authority from God.

Some called him Bishop; others addressed him as Your Excellency; a few referred to him as The Boss; but almost everyone else affectionately knew him and remember him as simply "Our Jerry."

I have always felt both affection and loyalty toward Bishop Minihan for one everlasting reason. It was he who confirmed me during the mid-1950s, and it was through him that I received the grace and strength of the Holy Spirit to become a mature Christian.

Part Two

The Men of Sports

Harry Agganis

Baseball Heroes Are Not Supposed to Die

Monday, June 27, 1955 was an unusually hot and humid early summer day in Greater Boston. The temperature flirted with ninety degrees as I bounced a tennis ball off the front steps of our house. A neighbor driving down the street, stopped and rolled down the window.

"Harry Agganis died! I just heard the news on the radio!" he shouted.

Despite the heat, I felt a chill.

It was early afternoon, sometime between noon and one o'clock. I was already dressed in my Little League baseball uniform, even though the first pitch of my game would not be thrown until shortly after six that evening.

At the time, I was in a hurry. Being in my uniform five hours before the game was typical of me. I was always in a rush for more baseball. My life was a succession of line drives, pop-ups and ground balls. Mine was the innocent world of back-hand stabs, tumbling one-handed catches, bubble gum, baseball cards and digging into a batter's box which had been marked off by dragging the barrel-end of a bat over the dirt. But as the reality of death intruded on my innocent world, I changed.

I was only eleven years old. Harry Agganis was my hero. He was the twenty-six year old first baseman for the Boston Red Sox and a former All-American quarterback for Coach Buff Donelli's Boston University Terriers. It never occurred to me that my hero could die. A boy's hero never dies. Does he? Sadly, Harry did indeed die, and today he has been dead for over four decades.

At eleven years old, I was wild about baseball. Some people, including my mother, were convinced I had no other interests. As I look back at that period in my life, I must admit that they were right.

Despite my fondness for baseball, I was never crazy about the Red Sox. In fact, I was weaned on the Boston Braves. When the Braves packed their tepees and headed to Milwaukee in 1953, I felt like my best friend had pulled up stakes and moved to the Midwest. So before he could become my hero, Harry had to overcome my lukewarm feelings about the Red Sox. He did. And thanks to Harry, I could almost forgive the Braves for abandoning me. Infatuation has a way of healing wounds, at least when you are young.

As a boy, I actually had two heroes. My first was Phil Masi, a battle-worn catcher for the Braves who wore number 10. He grew up in Chicago. He is best remembered for an incident in the first game of the 1948 World Series between the Braves and the Cleveland Indians. He was picked off at second base by Bob Feller, but umpire Bill Stewart ruled him safe. Moments later, Masi scored the winning run on a single by Tommy Holmes, as the Braves and Johnny Sain defeated the Indians and Bob Feller, 1-0, at Braves Field. The Cleveland Tribe won the Series in six games. They have not won a World Series since.

Numbers. My favorite is 5. Agganis wore number 6 for the Red Sox. When he was playing quarterback and putting Boston University on the big-time college football map, he wore 33 on his scarlet B.U. jersey. At the time, I was a shortstop, not a catcher or a first baseman. No one ever stated that rationality has anything to do with how boys select their heroes.

I was short, chubby and covered with freckles. My eyes are blue, and once-upon-a-time I had light brown hair. Masi was a stocky, dark-complexioned Italian. Agganis was Greek, and I am Irish. Harry was 6-foot-1, 190-pounds, a terrific physical specimen. He was left-handed; I am right-handed. Harry had jet black hair, olive-tinted skin and perfect teeth, whiter than freshly fallen snow. His nickname was the "Golden Greek." I didn't like my nickname, "Wally," although I warmed up to it after hearing about Wally Post, the ex-power-hitting outfielder who played for the Cincinnati Reds. It also didn't hurt that the star of the "Leave it to Beaver" TV series had an older brother who was also named Wally.

But when you are eleven years old and your twenty-six year old hero dies, nightmares become more than just bad dreams. They take on a daily reality. Even Disneyland loses its magic.

The day after Harry died, one of the Boston daily newspapers, the old Record-American, ran a photograph of Harry's aged and widowed mother bending over his casket and kissing her youngest child. It terrified me. I was so frightened that I covered my eyes to avoid looking at the photo, which covered almost the entire page of the tabloid newspaper.

"Harry didn't really die!" I kept telling myself. For a moment, I convinced myself that his death was just a bad dream. Then, the thought of that photograph brought me back to a reality from which there was no escape. Harry was gone. Forever. For me, that meant he would still be dead tomorrow and the day after.

At the time of Harry's death, the Red Sox were in Washington playing the Senators. I listened to the game on the radio. There was a special pregame tribute to Harry, and Hall of Fame Broadcaster Curt Gowdy eulogized him. Years later, Gowdy told me during an interview that Harry and Ted Williams were the two most unforgettable athletes he had met.

Courtesy of Boston University

1951: Boston University quarterback Harry Agannis running with the ball.

As I listened to the radio broadcast from the nation's capital, I became angry and frustrated. "How can they play baseball without Harry?" I asked myself. "It's not fair," I answered. "No one should ever play baseball again."

For a long time after Harry died, I was petrified of death. I was an altar boy, but I refused to serve at funeral Masses. Daily, I walked past our church, Our Lady Help of Christians, on my way to the playground. If there was a funeral, I took an alternate route so I would not have to pass the church. I feared hearses and I despised anything and everything black, especially the black armbands the Red Sox wore throughout the remainder of the 1955 season in memory of Harry.

Harry, who broke in with the Red Sox in 1954, was hitting .313 before he became sick in early May and was admitted to the hospital for the first time. However, he appeared to have recovered from a severe bout with bronchitis and rejoined the team after spending a week in the hospital.

On a road trip, he belted a double at the old Comisky Park in Chicago against the White Sox. It was his final big-league hit. From Chicago, the Red Sox traveled to Kansas City by train. Trainer Jack Fadden, who also was the Harvard trainer, heard Harry coughing and gasping for air in the middle of the night as the train rattled across the Midwest. Shortly after the team arrived in Kansas City, Harry was sent home and was readmitted to the hospital.

Once again, this time after a ten day stay, he appeared to be recovering. The night before he died, Sunday, June 26, 1955, a friend visited him, and Harry waved to family members from the window in his hospital room.

He died the next morning just before noon. The cause of death was a blood clot. He had pneumonia, and his overall condition was complicated by phlebitis. As a boy, he had respiratory problems. Some theorized that the beating he took in a college football game against Maryland hastened his death. Mystery surrounded his death then, and it still does. Today, modern medicine probably could have saved his life.

Harry chose baseball over pro football. He was the number one draft choice of the Cleveland Browns. One reason he selected baseball over football was to stay close to his family, particularly his mother. The family home was in Lynn, a short distance from Boston and Fenway Park.

One time, prior to a game at Fenway Park, Harry spotted his aging mother in the stands. She had just arrived and was struggling to get to her seat. Immediately, Harry rushed over to the edge of the stands and in full uniform, vaulted over the barrier and headed toward his mother. He personally took her hand and led her to her seat. Then, he scolded the ushers for not being alert and not taking better care of his mother.

He was Hollywood handsome. He dated beauty queens and had his own fan club when he was still a schoolboy. He was loyal and dedicated to his family and friends. He had a million dollar smile and a magnetic personality. He was proud of his heritage, which included the Greek Orthodox faith. Everyone loved Harry Agganis. "There was a sweetness about him," remarked Curt Gowdy. "My wife and I were crushed when he died. We both loved him."

The "sweetness" came from his faith in God. Mary Trank worked for the Red Sox for thirty years. She was an executive assistant to former owner Tom Yawkey and general manager Dick O'Connell. She first met Harry when he was a student-athlete at Boston University.

Harry walked from B.U. to Fenway Park where he occasionally visited Mary in her office. "He was so polite, always a gentleman," said Mary, who is now retired and lives in Waltham, Massachusetts.

During visits, Agganis told Mary how badly he wanted to make the Red Sox team. "He was real nervous about the challenge, and he didn't want to fail," she said, recalling their conversations.

Mary told Agganis to pray. She even explained the Catholic devotion known as a novena to him, and she promised to say a special novena for Harry's intentions. He thanked her and promised to start praying a novena himself.

Agganis had to return to school to complete credits after he signed a baseball contract with the Red Sox. On the day Harry graduated from Boston University, he hit a home run against the Philadelphia Athletics, changed his clothes, and then rushed down Commonwealth Avenue to receive his college diploma.

"Harry was wonderful, just so refreshing," said Mary. "I can still feel the pain all of us felt when he died."

Years after, the late Paul Brown, coach and founder of the Cleveland Browns, told me during an interview, "If Harry had chosen to play football, he could have become the greatest pro quarterback that ever played the game."

Around the time of his death, rumors circulated about him playing both pro football and baseball, although the Red Sox most likely never would have given him permission to play both sports.

For me, his death was my moment of passage. It changed something inside me. After Harry died, I was never a little boy again.

Ernie Banks—"Mr. Cub"

Mr. Cub

From the very beginning, Ernie Banks was paid to play baseball. As a youngster, Ernie had little interest in the game. He got his start in the sport only after his father agreed to pay him twenty-five cents just to play catch. It might have been the wisest investment Mr. Banks ever made, because Ernie's natural ability was just waiting to develop.

Banks was on the roster of the Kansas City Monarchs of the old Negro League when he joined the Cubs in September of 1953. He hit his first major league home run on September 20, 1953. By the time he retired from baseball in 1971, he had a total of 512 career home runs.

He has a vivid memory of the greeting he received from Jackie Robinson, a fellow African-American who, just a few years earlier in 1947, broke the color barrier that had ruled major league baseball since the beginning.

"We were playing the Dodgers, and Jackie came running across the field to greet me," recalled Banks.

"Glad to see you. Great to have you with us," Robinson told him on the first day the Hall of Famers met in the big leagues.

"Jackie told me to keep my ears open and to listen, because if I did, I would learn a lot," recalled Banks. "And he also said, 'You are going to do fine, just fine.' Jackie's encouragement really helped."

Ernie played nineteen seasons in the big leagues, all with the Cubs. He was the first African-American to play for the team and the first Cubs player to have his number (14) retired. A career .274 hitter, he was a steady and sturdy ballplayer, the first home-run hitting shortstop of the modern era, and later a slugging first baseman. He had four monster seasons with the Cubs, including back-to-back seasons (1958 and 1959) when he was named the National League Most Valuable Player.

In 1955, Banks batted .295 with 44 homers and 117 runs batted in. In 1958, he batted .313, hit 47 homers, and drove in 129 runs. In 1959, he batted .304, with 45 homers and 143 RBIs. Then, in 1960, he hit .271 with 41 homers and 117 RBIs.

Banks may never have lasted so long in the majors if it was not for concerned friends. During his prime, Ernie was listed at 6-foot-1, 180 pounds, but he had difficulty maintaining his weight. In fact, once, during the dog days of summer, Phil Wrigley, owner of the Cubs, ordered Ernie to stay home and rest rather than make a trip to Milwaukee where the Cubs were scheduled to play the Braves.

"My weight got down to 159 pounds," said Banks. "When I got to the big leagues, I had to learn how eat properly. I was used to eating one meal a day, practically starving myself."

Umpire Emmett Ashford, the first African-American to call balls and strikes in the big leagues, and teammate Gene Baker, who played second base for the Cubs and was a close friend, took Banks aside and told him he had to bulk up on the groceries if he wanted to last in the big leagues. "They force-fed me malted milk shakes," said Ernie, smiling as he spoke. "I started eating breakfast. The Cubs played all home games during the day, so there was plenty of time after the game to go out and get a real good meal."

Banks grew up in Dallas. He is the second oldest and first son in a family of twelve children. His parents, Eddie and Essie, were hard-working, humble people. His father, a jack of all trades, could do anything. His mother ran the home and she taught her children the importance of prayer.

"I never forgot that," said Ernie. "My mother always prayed. When I started hitting home runs in the big league, I knew I wasn't doing it alone. As I rounded the bases, I often looked up and said, 'Thank you, Jesus.' "

When you first meet Ernie, it is impossible not to notice his sparkling eyes, unwrinkled, baby-smooth skin and his mammoth hands, as large as a pair of bushel baskets. "I developed strong hands by picking cotton on my hands and knees," he said.

When he was young, he was painfully shy and introverted. "I wasn't much of a talker," he said.

As a ballplayer, he let his overflowing ability do the talking for him. Although he was as quiet as a church mouse, he was known for his sunshine disposition as well as the joy he exhibited just playing baseball. Always a gentleman, always an ambassador for the game, he never argued with umpires and he always carried himself with dignity and grace. In fact, that is how he got the nickname "Mr. Cub."

Jim Enright, a Chicago sports writer who, during the winter officiated Big Ten college basketball games, nicknamed Ernie "Mr. Cub" primarily because of his gentlemanly manner. The two, in fact, became close friends. "He was a great champion of mine," said Ernie, "a true angel in my life."

Many probably do not remember that Banks had a scare during the 1956 season. He developed a blister on his glove hand. "I probably got it from holding the bat too tight," explained Ernie. In those days, hitters did not wear batting gloves.

Well, the blister soon became badly infected, so much so that his hand became swollen like a balloon, and his arm turned blue up to the elbow. Finally, he was taken to the emergency room. A doctor who was going off duty walked by, took one look at Banks' hand and arm and rushed him in for immediate treatment.

The quick action saved Ernie's life. "The doctor told me that if I had waited much longer I would have died," said Ernie, recalling the frightening incident.

Banks remained in the hospital for days. One teammate visited him. The player's name was Monte Irvin, the Hall of Fame outfielder. Irvin, the former New York Giants' great, finished his big-league career with the Cubs in 1956, hitting a modest .271 in 111 games. Irvin had his best season for the National League Champion Giants in 1951, the year of Bobby Thomson's epic pennant-clinching home run against the Dodgers in a playoff game at the old Polo Grounds—"The shot heard around the world." In 1951, Irvin hit .312, smashed 24 home runs and drove in 121 runs.

"Monte and his wife came to visit me in the hospital," said Banks. "He is one of the few people I have met in my life I would call a near-perfect human being. He is a warm, wonderful man and he truly cares about people."

Despite his personal heroics, Ernie played on many dismal Cub teams, ball clubs that finished sixth, seventh and even eighth in an eight-team league. In 1969, the Cubs made a run at the National League East title and even held a seven-game lead over the Mets as late as August. But the Miracle Mets of '69 overtook the Cubs and went on to win the World Series, beating the heavily favored Baltimore Orioles.

Disappointed? Of course. Crushed? Not hardly. "I try to find good in everything," said Banks. "Even our collapse in '69 when everyone thought it was the Cubs' year to win the pennant."

Experience has taught Banks many things and with aging often comes wisdom. "Nothing in this life, except death and taxes, is in the bag," said Ernie. "Sometimes when you win, you actually lose; and sometimes when you lose, you actually win. The spiritual is the only thing that lasts."

When he was a young player, Banks took out insurance that made him financially secure when his playing career was over. As a player, he never made more than $55,000 in a single season. "The major thrust of me playing baseball was never about money," said Banks.

The lure was love of the game, and the classy Banks produced many thrilling moments, both for him and baseball fans all across the country. In the 1960 All-Star game at Municipal Stadium in Kansas City, where he had played for the Kansas City Monarchs, he clouted a two-run first-inning home run off Bill Monbouquette of the Red Sox, a blast that helped spark the National League to a 5-3 victory over the American League.

"What pitch did you hit out?" Banks was asked.

"It was a high slider," he replied.

The blast was especially gratifying to Jack Quinlan, who broadcast the game on radio that day, July 11, 1960. Prior to the game, Quinlan had implored Ernie by saying: "Do something early in the game, Ernie, because I am broadcasting the first few innings."

Banks became the Cubs' regular shortstop in 1954. For eight seasons, he was the only power-hitting shortstop in baseball during an era that produced great shortstops such as Pee Wee Reese (Dodgers), Roy MacMillan (Reds), Alvin Dark (Giants), Dick Groat (Pirates), Johnny Logan (Braves) and Phil Rizzuto (Yankees), just to name six, all of whom were singles hitters, players who sprayed the ball to all fields.

Today, three of the game's glamour shortstops—Nomar Garciaparra, Derek Jeter and Alex Rodriquez—are known for both their flashy gloves and the long-ball thump in their bat. "They would be stars during any era," said Banks, about the trio. However, long before any of the three were born, slugger Ernie Banks set the standard for power-hitting short-stops.

Banks has had his share of ups and downs. The father of three children, including twins, he has been married three times. He is a man who looks for the positive in life. "I have tried to live above and beyond," he said. "And that includes all the racial stuff."

Today, Banks works to raise awareness of the dangers of high blood pressure for a national education campaign called "Have a Heart," a program geared to raise awareness of the dangers of hypertension. Once Banks discovered he had high blood pressure, successful treatment has enabled Ernie to manage the disease and live a normal, active life.

Ernie established the Ernie Banks Foundation, which assists primarily elders and inner-city children. From hitting home runs to going to bat to fight the dangers of high blood pressure, Ernie Banks continues to make a difference. And he does it in his trademark soft-spoken yet enthusiastic manner.

A final note. The fact that Banks would some times look to heaven and say, "Thank you, Jesus" as he circled the bases after hitting a home run, evokes a rather simple adage: "You can't be hateful, if you're grateful."

Perhaps that is why Ernie Banks earned his sobriquet, "Mr. Cub."

Bob Cousy

The Cooz

He still lives in Worcester, Massachusetts, not far from the College of the Holy Cross where he unveiled his basketball wizardry more than fifty years ago, and a mere tricky dribble from the Basketball Hall of Fame in nearby Springfield, where he is forever enshrined as "Mr. Basketball."

More than anyone else, Bob Cousy transformed basketball from Dr. James Naismith's sluggish, set-shot slow dance of yesterday to today's start-your-engines, above-the-rim, razzle-dazzle spectacle.

It is hard to believe that The Cooz is now in his mid-seventies. But it has been four decades since "Number 14" dribbled behind his back for the Boston Celtics, swished a one-hand set shot, skipped down the lane and scored on a running hook shot, or flipped a drop pass to a teammate cutting to the basket.

Bob Cousy was born just months after his parents passed through Ellis Island on their way from France to the United States. He spent most of his youth on Manhattan's Lower East Side "right where the ghettos are today along the East River," he said.

Joseph Cousy, his father, drove a cab. Juliette, his mother, was a house-wife. When he was twelve, the family moved to a new home. "My father worked eighteen-hour days and managed to save $500 to put down on a little place on Long Island...to give us some air," said Cousy.

Cousy had one sibling, a half-sister, Blanche, from his father's first marriage. His father's first wife died of tuberculosis. Blanche remained in France and was raised by relatives. Cousy did not meet her until she came to the United States many years later. Like Cousy, his half-sister was a natural athlete.

"She played basketball for the French national team," reported Cousy. "She was a champion cyclist. She managed a resort hotel. She was a physiotherapist, and she fought for the French Resistance during World War II."

Courtesy of Holy Cross College

Holy Cross Crusader Bob Cousy flies towards the hoop.

Then Cousy added, "There must have been good athletic genes on my father's side of the family."

Long before Cousy outfoxed the defensive tactics of old NBA rivals such as Slater Martin (Minneapolis Lakers), Larry Costello (Syracuse Nationals), Bob Davies (Rochester Royals) and brothers Al and Dick McGuire (New York Knicks), he had to overcome deep feelings of insecurity as an only child of immigrant parents.

"I wouldn't say my family background was exactly normal," said Cousy. "There was just me. There were no relatives coming over on holidays; they were all back in France. I was shy and retiring. Sports saved me. You wouldn't say I came charging out of the big city ready to take on the world."

Cousy grew up during an era when athletics were pure, unspoiled and college recruiting was unsophisticated. He wound up at Holy Cross, but he almost enrolled at another Jesuit institution, rival Boston College.

"There were no dorms at Boston College," said Cousy. "They told me they would put me up with a nice family. I was a shy French kid from New York. That idea scared the heck out of me, so I went to Holy Cross where I could hide in a dormitory."

Eventually, however, Cousy made it to Boston College. From 1963-69, he was the head basketball coach, guiding the Eagles to a 117-38 record.

Interestingly, the French kid from New York, who spoke a foreign language at home, still has difficulty pronouncing the English 'r' sound. "I don't know if the problem is caused by New York slang or New England twang," said Cousy, laughing as he spoke.

Regardless, a string of r's in a name or phrase can really rattle The Cooz. "I get letters all the time about my diction and grammar," said Cousy, who for years has been a color commentator on Boston Celtics' televised games. "Remember when Rick Robey played for the Celtics? I butchered his name."

His nasal, rolling r's caused a problem when it came to pronouncing his future wife's name, Marie. When he first met her, he could not pronounce Marie, so he called her Missy, a nickname she picked up from her brothers.

Like her husband, Marie Ritterbusch Cousy is from New York. She said she knew Bob for eight years before they were married, and he always enjoyed the warmth of her extended family. "My family—even the aunts, the uncles, and the cousins—have always been responsive to him," she said. "Over the years, they have had a special relationship."

Cousy has cultivated lasting relationships with many different people during his life, including a nun, Sister Mary Patricia, SCH (Sisters of Charity of Halifax). She also happened to be Cousy's kindergarten teacher. Periodically, Cousy visits her at the retirement home where she lives.

"Sister is a real go-getter," said Cousy. "One time she brought me down to the cafeteria. Before I had a chance to stop her, she announced to all the other sisters: 'Look who I have with me, Bob Cousy!' "

Bob Cousy is a basketball legend. More important, he is a man blessed with deep faith in God. "Life can be tough," said Cousy. "Even the agnostics and atheists wake up and find themselves crying in the night. Faith in God is very important, particularly when you get to be my age."

The Cousys are members of Blessed Sacrament parish, and their two daughters attended the parish school in Worcester.

Jet Commercial Photographers

Coach Cousy (front left) with his 1968-1969 Boston College squad. Jim O'Brien, former B.C. and current Ohio State head coach is number 10 (back row, third from left).

Although Cousy does not have a favorite devotion or prayer, he begins each day by raising his heart and mind to God. "I look up at the ceiling and say: 'Thank you, God, for another day and for all my blessings.' "

Cousy's one regret is that his basketball career relegated him to the role of absentee father much of the time. "I got caught up in the jock thing, of playing and coaching," he said. "I missed so much when the girls were growing up. My wife did it all. She devoted her entire life to our daughters."

Marie Cousy does not agree. Instead, she applauds her husband for paying the price to achieve greatness in his profession. "Sure he was away," said Mrs. Cousy, "but that was his job, what he chose to do. He gave so much of himself and worked so hard. You don't become an exceptional player and win all those championships without that kind of dedication."

Cousy's fabulous NBA career began inauspiciously after his name was reluctantly picked out of a hat by the Boston Celtics. He signed his first pro contract in 1950 for a meager $9,000. Nevertheless, he is not resentful of the millions that today's superstars are paid. "The lottery picks get $33 million," he pointed out, "but I'm not the least bit envious."

As a player, he is a legend, probably the NBA's first genuine superstar (along with George Mikan). The six-foot-one Cousy, with unusually long arms, a thin upper body and oak-tree thick legs, was elected to the Basketball Hall of Fame in 1970. He also was selected to the NBA's twenty-fifth and thirty-fifth anniversary all-star teams. He was the league's most valuable player in 1957 as well as the MVP of the 1954 and 1957 All-Star games. He was a magician with the basketball, and his floor leadership led the Boston Celtics to six NBA championships.

The Cooz also scored 16,960 points and dished out 6,955 assists during his career. He averaged 18.4 points per game during the regular season and 18.5 during the playoffs. He was so popular that every kid on the block—youngsters like me—who dribbled a basketball dreamed of someday becoming another Bob Cousy.

Once, when I was about ten years old, I managed to get Cousy's autograph. It was during the first game of an NBA doubleheader—the Syracuse Nationals versus the New York Knicks in the first game—at the old Boston Garden. I managed to slip away from my father and sneak down to the main lobby. I walked down a long, dark tunnel and waited. I was alone. A figure approached from far away. As he got closer, I was startled when I recognized who it was—Bob Cousy arriving in street clothes for the game later that evening against the Minneapolis Lakers.

Although he was only six-foot-one, to me, Cousy seemed about ten feet tall. Nervously, I went up to him. "Bob, could I please have your autograph?" I asked in a stutter.

"Sure, son," he replied.

I remember my thoughts at the time: "Wow, for a few seconds I had Bob Cousy all to myself in a corner of a dark and dingy Boston Garden corridor. Just The Cooz, me and a hidden rat or two. I can't wait to tell my buddies and show them the autograph."

Years ago, I lost the autograph, but never the memory.

How big was Bob Cousy? What he did not know then is that at the time I wished I had darker skin so I could have had dark hair on my legs, like he had, instead of blond peach fuzz; and when I shot baskets by myself, I wore a white undershirt, on the front and back of which I drew a green number 14 with magic marker. Back then, zillions of kids in the greater Boston area all wanted to be "Rapid Robert Cousy," one of the many nicknames that the late Johnny Most, the great Celtics' radio voice, pinned on The Cooz.

Speaking of memories, some never fade in terms of where you were and what were you were doing during significant moments in history. I was on guard duty for the U.S. Army in Germany in 1963 when I learned that John F. Kennedy had been assassinated; I was inside a gin mill on Cape Cod drinking dime draft beers in the summer of 1969 on the day man first walked on the moon; and I was sitting in a car during the winter of 1965 listening to Most's radio broadcast the night "Havlicek Stole The Ball," preserving the Celtics' playoff victory over Wilt Chamberlain and Philadelphia.

Incidentally, always a huge Celtics fan, I was there, sitting in the first row of the second balcony at the Boston Garden in December 1956, the day that Bill Russell played his first game for the Celtics against the St. Louis Hawks. Immediately, Cousy and Russell established a bond that continues to this very day.

Both on and off the court, Cousy has always demonstrated compassion for minorities and others less fortunate. "Bob always understood the plight of the black man," said Father John Brooks, S.J., president emeritus of Holy Cross College. "He believes that every person, regardless of race or religion, is a child of God."

Father Brooks also praised Cousy for the depth of his faith. "He is very idealistic about his faith," continued Father Brooks, who has been a friend for years. "His beliefs have grown out of his commitment to the Catholic faith. It is a faith he cherishes."

Father Brooks also said that Cousy has been a leader in Big Brother and Big Sister organizations since his playing days, serving as national director in 1964-65. "He has personally gotten involved and helped so many underprivileged children," said Father Brooks.

As for the world around him, Cousy decries the lack of decency and civility. "Just turn on the television day or night and what you see is misery and heartache everywhere," he said. "At the root of our problems are the breakdown of moral values and the family. Despite all the sophistication of living in this age, the human animal has not learned how to live peacefully together."

To combat cynicism, Cousy receives inspiration from modern day heroes, caring people who demonstrate compassion, character and integrity, idealists like the late tennis great Arthur Ashe. "He was a positive force for good," said Cousy.

While many long-time basketball buffs think they know all about "Mr. Basketball"—like the night he scored fifty points during a four overtime 111-105 playoff victory over the Syracuse Nationals in March 1953—there is much about Cousy that he keeps private.

For instance, he worked in the Catskills as a waiter to help put himself through college. He wrote his senior college thesis on the persecution of minorities. After graduating from Holy Cross, he and teammate Frank Oftring pumped gas and started a driver education school. He had a bout with diverticulitis that required surgery.

Incidentally, his wife, Missy, says that he is easy to live with and The Cooz even took up piano several years ago. "I took piano lessons to help me relax," said Cousy. "I quit when it became pressure...when the piano lessons reached the choking point."

Photograph by Bill Smith, Chicago, IL

Mike Ditka

Iron Mike

M ike Ditka likes being compared to the commander of allied forces in the Persian Gulf War—the "Stormin' Norman" Schwartzkopf among coaches in the National Football League.

Had he not been a head football coach, Ditka probably would have made a heck of a general. It is easy to envision him as a career military man with stars on his battle helmet, an infantry soldier's closest comrade, a combat veteran who dreads war, yet forever extols the virtues of duty, honor, God and country.

But Mike Ditka's top command posts have been head coaching jobs in the National Football League. In his first head coaching job he brought the Chicago Bears back to prominence. He then commanded the New Orleans Saints, previously known as "The Aints"—the only NFL team that had never won a playoff game. But his efforts to change their history were unsuccessful.

Mike Ditka is tough with a Capital T, yet he is a man of deep contrition who knows his weaknesses and turns to God for forgiveness.

Ditka was born the first of four children in Carnegie, Pennsylvania, on October 18, 1939. He was raised in Aliquippa, a steel mill town of 30,000 people about twenty miles from Pittsburgh. His father, Mike (the original family name was Dyzco), came from Ukrainian stock. His mother, Charlotte Keller, traced her ancestry to both Germany and Ireland.

Mike's father worked at a back-breaking trade, repairing railroad cars. He was a disciplinarian who ruled the Ditka home with an iron fist. Young Mike learned the difference between right and wrong at an early age—the hard way. "My father kicked my butt," said Ditka, "and thank God he did!"

Mike's mother, a Catholic convert, oversaw her son's religious education. "She made sure I learned my catechism lessons," Ditka says.

As a youth, Ditka served as an altar boy, and he attended St. Titus School through the eighth grade. During that formative time in his life, he was surrounded by positive role models. The list included parish priests, the Sisters of St. Joseph and his coaches. And as a kid playing sandlot baseball, he had another positive role model—Hall of Fame baseball player Stan Musial.

Ditka remembers two men who had a special influence on him. One was Father Francis Plante, a priest at St. Titus School. The other was Carl Aschman, his football coach at Aliquippa High School. "They gave me encouragement and they also made sure I stayed on the straight and narrow," said Ditka.

Aschman was an immigrant from Turkey who played college football at Washington and Jefferson University in Washington, Pennsylvania. He later coached at Aliquippa High School from 1941 until he retired in 1964. To Ditka, Aschman was a man who had deep faith in God and used a game—football—to inspire boys to lift their visions above and beyond the smoke stacks of the local steel mills. He died on Thanksgiving Day 1971.

"He was a strong man and he was a good man," said Ditka. "Coach Aschman went to Mass and Communion every morning. As tough as he was, he really cared about us. We respected him, although we moaned and grumbled about some of the things he did."

Frank Marocco and Ditka were teammates at Aliquippa High School. Today, Marocco is the head football coach at Aliquippa, also known as the "Fighting Quips." To illustrate just how tough Aschman was, Marocco says: "When Coach Aschman told you to be home by 9:00 P.M., you sat by the telephone and looked out the window, just in case he drove by your house."

Ditka was a football player's football player. He was an All-American at the University of Pittsburgh and was later named to the pro football Hall of

Fame. He redefined the tight end position while playing for the Bears, the Philadelphia Eagles and the Dallas Cowboys. Iron Mike, as he came to be known, branded the game with his own passion. He was a gifted athlete who played with the temperament of a wild boar. He was a blocker and a pass receiver who acted like he was a linebacker. Ditka attacked opponents in frequent fits of controlled rage.

Old number 89's natural fury was a perfect match for a collision game like football. "He always had that intensity," said Marocco. "It probably goes back to his childhood, from the struggle of having to be tougher than everybody else. He grew up with violence all around him, even though he had a stable family life.

"No one took any crap around the Linmar Housing Plan, where five or six families lived in one unit. The only way you survived was by kicking someone's butt before you got yours kicked."

Ditka retired as an active player in 1972, but, at some level, he will always be a football player. "Mike has never stopped playing the game," said Marocco. "All that pent-up anger exploded on the football field. He still feels the contact. He's still making the crunching block, that big run and that bone-crushing tackle. That's why he's able to get inside of each player."

To the people of Aliquippa, Ditka stands taller than the old smoke stacks that rise above the steel mills. Every June, Mike returns home and hosts the Mike Ditka Golf Tournament which

Courtesy of University of Pittsburgh Media Relations

Ditka playing for the University of Pittsburgh Panthers.

raises $10,000 for the high school's scholarship fund. "No one generates excitement around here the way Mike Ditka does," said Marocco. "He is a hero. People just want to shake his hand, take his picture and just be around him."

Instead of an annual banquet, Ditka prefers a Texas-style barbecue. "We have a tent the size of a football field," said Marocco. "Mike likes to mingle with the people while everyone eats roast lamb, roast pig. They wash it all down with ice cold beer and a shot or two of whiskey."

Ditka was known to utter profanity, often in machine gun fashion. But before his second season as head coach of the Saints, he decided to clean up his language. He is convinced, however, that God does not keep score of his improper and less-than-holy utterances. "I'm not going to hell for saying a four letter word," said Ditka, several years ago. That was before a conversion experience made him determined to sweeten the sounds that come out of his mouth.

Photo by Bill Smith, Chicago, IL

On the sidelines for the Chicago Bears

Despite his gruff exterior, Ditka is a sensitive man. "I believe in the Golden Rule," he said, "and I am going to be judged by how much compassion I had in my heart for my fellow man, how much I cared, and how well I related to others."

The mercurial Ditka knows that some may judge him severely. "People see me ranting and raving on the sidelines, and they probably say, "Hey, that guy is no Christian; he's nuts, he's crazy," said Ditka.

Since he suffered a heart attack in 1988 at age forty-eight, Mike cherishes quiet time in the morning. He swims, works out on a treadmill, pumps weights, runs wind sprints and then calms himself down with prayer. Prayer and contemplation are a perfect balance for an intensely driven competitor like Mike.

> Despite his gruff exterior, Ditka is a sensitive man. "I believe in the Golden Rule," he said, "and I am going to be judged by how much compassion I had in my heart for my fellow man, how much I cared, and how well I related to others."

"I don't pray for myself," he explained. "I never have. My prayer is one of thanksgiving for all I have been given and for the gift of life itself. I also pray for the souls in purgatory and I ask for the intercession of the Blessed Mother."

"Why do you pray?" the burly football great was asked.

"I do it because I believe it and because the Church teaches me to do it," he said.

He also attends weekly Mass and regularly participates in a daily liturgy throughout the year, especially during Lent.

During his years as a player and as an assistant coach with the Dallas Cowboys, Ditka and his wife, Diana, reached a crossroads in their faith journey. Diana explained, "Mike was restless, and he was searching for something, but he didn't know what."

At the suggestion of former Cowboys' coach Tom Landry, a committed Christian, the Ditkas began attending Bible classes. "I knew in my head that Jesus died for our sins, but I didn't know it in my heart until Mike and I started studying the Bible with others," said Diana.

Around that same time, while driving on the LBJ Highway in Dallas, Mike received a scare that heightened his awareness of God as well as his own mortality. "Mike was almost killed," reported Diana. "He drove off the highway on the wrong exit ramp and two tractor trailers nearly ran him over. At the last second, a terrible accident was somehow averted."

Ditka was so shaken by the near-accident that when he returned home he still was ashen. "The first thing he said was, 'There must be a reason for me to be here,'" said Diana.

Diana shared that Mike is a giving person. She also said that, although he can flare quickly, he also apologizes almost immediately. "He is the first person to admit he is wrong and to say he is sorry," said Diana. "Mike does not hold grudges either."

For much of his life, Iron Mike waged a knock-down, drag-out war with himself trying to cap the fires that raged within. Time and the grace of self-acceptance have dimmed the flame, although no one will ever call Mike Ditka mellow. "Mike is happy with himself," said Diana. "He shares much more of himself with the family, and he is even able to say, 'I love you.' "

Mike says that his personal growth has made him more comfortable with himself and more accepting of others. "I still get disappointed, but I don't get as angry as I once did," he said.

Nevertheless, Ditka becomes incensed when he is criticized for his beliefs, particularly his opposition to abortion. "Everything is washed over today—not exactly right and not exactly wrong," he said. "Abortion is murder. If I believe something is morally wrong and against the laws of God, I am going to say so. That is my right and my duty. The most courageous thing anyone can do is stand up for what they believe. Look at the Apostles. Peter was crucified upside down for what he believed."

Ditka coached the Bears for eleven seasons. In 1985, his Bears ran roughshod over the league, posted a 15-1 regular season record and crushed the Patriots in the Super Bowl 46-10 to become world champions.

After a stint as an NFL television analyst, Mike returned to coaching in 1999. He spent three years with the New Orleans Saints compiling a record of 15 wins and 33 losses. He was fired at the end of his third season.

Today, Mike Ditka owns a restaurant in Chicago and works as an NFL analyst on radio and television. He enjoys his family, plays gin rummy and golfs with his buddies. Whenever he is perplexed about anything—a missed tackle, a sliced tee shot or even having to answer his own telephone while his secretary is on vacation—Iron Mike Ditka cherishes and finds comfort in the words from St. Paul's letter to the Philippians (4:13): "In him who is the source of my strength, I have strength for everything."

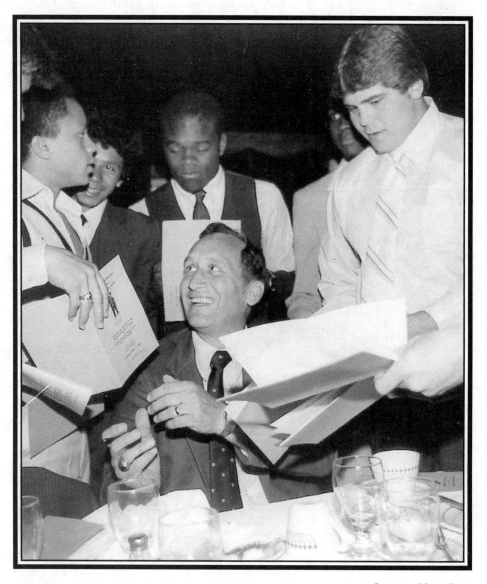

Gerry Faust
at Boys Town, Omaha, Nebraska

The Ecstasy and the Agony

During a visit to the South Bend, Indiana, campus of Notre Dame, Gerry Faust, the head football coach at Moeller High School in Cincinnati, Ohio, petitioned the Blessed Mother for a favor.

At the time, Faust and his family attended Notre Dame's annual spring intra-squad game. While at Notre Dame, Gerry first stopped at the famous grotto to Our Lady where he prayed, concluding with a special request: "If you intercede by helping me become the Notre Dame football coach," prayed Faust, "I will visit you here at the grotto every day."

Within three weeks Faust, the head coach of the most successful high school football program in the country, was contacted by Notre Dame and, to the surprise of almost everyone, he soon became the twenty-fourth head football coach of the Fighting Irish. Faust replaced Dan Devine, who was forced to resign because of his wife's poor health.

During his five years (1981-85) as head coach, 1,825 days during which Gerry was severely tested, Faust kept his promise. Some days he made more than one trip to the grotto. On other occasions, when Notre Dame returned home from a road game, Faust always went out of his way to pray at the grotto, even if it happened to be three o'clock in the morning.

Despite much fanfare and soaring expectations, Faust resigned after five seasons. There was little satisfaction in the fact that his teams, during that span, lost fifteen games by eight or fewer points. If he had not resigned, he would have been fired. His five year record was 30-26-1, too close to mediocrity for the ghosts of Notre Dame's illustrious past or to overcome scathing criticism from the press and grumbling from alumni—all of whom were very much alive at the time Gerry walked away from the dream job of his football-coaching life.

He made the decision to resign after the next to last game of his final season, a 10-7 loss to LSU. In his final game, Notre Dame and its lame duck coach were crushed by the University of Miami [Florida] Hurricanes, 58-7.

Late in the LSU game, All-America Timmy Brown dropped a pass from quarterback Steve Beuerlein that would have given Notre Dame a first down at the LSU 15 yard line.

After the Fighting Irish lost, Brown, the future Oakland Raiders' star, was inconsolable. In fact, someone rushed up to Faust, who was still on the field, and told him, "You better get into the locker room. Timmy Brown is shaken up. He's crying his eyes out."

When Faust finally reached Brown, the player cried out, "I lost the game, Coach. I lost the game."

"No you didn't," Faust told him. "I made five or six questionable calls long before that, so your dropping a pass should not have mattered."

At that moment, Faust said he made the decision to resign. "I told myself," remembered Gerry. "This is not fair. I can't continue to put these kids through this type of suffering."

Three days later Gerry walked into the office of Father Edmund P. Joyce, C.S.C., Executive Vice President at Notre Dame, and told him that he had decided to resign. Immediately, the priest hugged him and said, "Coach, I was hoping you would do this."

In making the decision, Faust put what was best for the University ahead of his own interests. "I would never do anything to hurt Notre Dame," said a teary-eyed Faust at the time he stepped down. "It is obvious that the football program needs a change in direction."

Looking back, he said the decision he made was based on "common sense." "It wasn't happening," he said, "I wasn't getting the job done. I didn't want to have to put them [Notre Dame] through the agony of having to fire me."

In hindsight, Faust believes he probably put his first coaching staff together too hastily, tinkered with offense unnecessarily, and did not delegate responsibility as much as he should have. He also believes he should have been more aloof from the players. He says that he allowed himself to be too accessible and because of this he was not feared by his players.

But Gerry Faust is Gerry Faust. What you see is what you get. He wears no masks. When people meet him, they instinctively know they are meeting the genuine article, the real person. That is one of the main reasons why he has so many friends.

After resigning, Faust admitted that he was embarrassed and humbled. "It hurt more than anything I had ever experienced," he said.

But despite being humbled and embarrassed, Faust was not defeated. "Notre Dame is a great place," he said. "I loved every minute I spent there, but I didn't let it [his resigning] keep me down because I had my family, all the friends I made at Notre Dame and my faith to lean on."

For Faust, coaching football at Notre Dame was much more than a job. It was his mission, a personal crusade. The honor of coaching Notre Dame was an outward expression of Faust's burning desire to serve God as a teacher and a coach. "Gerry didn't coach at Notre Dame, he served there," said Faust's friend, Ken Schneider, an attorney from Cincinnati. "If Notre Dame called him today, he would go back in a second. His love for Notre Dame is that strong and that deep."

Despite the difficulty of choosing to walk away, Faust remains loyal to the University. "He still roots for Notre Dame," said Marlene, Gerry's wife.

Above all, Gerry is grateful that he had an opportunity to coach the Fighting Irish. He said he is a better man—more compassionate and more accepting of others—because of his coaching experience in South Bend.

If Faust became more accepting, not everyone was accepting of him. A case in point is Mark Bavaro, who played for Faust at Notre Dame and later became an all-pro tight end with the

Courtesy of University of Akron

At the University of Akron

New York Giants. Faust said that he and Bavaro, a deeply spiritual and equal-ly private man, had their differences. "He didn't like me," said Faust. "But I respect him, and it is his right if he feels that way. Mark was one of the toughest players I ever coached. He is hard to know and to understand. But he is genuine. There is not a phony bone in his body."

After leaving Notre Dame, Faust drew interest from Rice, Columbia, Marshall, Youngstown State and other schools. Finally, he accepted the head coaching position at Akron University, compiling a 43-53-3 record, including a personal best of 7-3-1 in 1992. During his tenure, Faust faced a different set of challenges than the ones he tackled at Notre Dame. During his tenure, the Akron football program was upgraded from Division 1AA to Division 1A, no easy task. "All of a sudden we started playing schools like Auburn and Tennessee," said Faust. "It was a challenge, a terrific opportunity."

However, in many ways, the cards were stacked against Faust at Akron. Faust felt that there were behind-the-scenes problems. He said he faced deception, jealousy and a lack of unity. Not everyone wanted Akron football and Faust to succeed, he said.

In 1994, after nine seasons, Akron fired Faust. The team had won just one game during that season. He was fired by the man he had recommended for the job of athletic director. "It was tough to take," Faust said. "But it was the greatest thing that has ever happened to me because of all I have been able to do since I left coaching."

Faust became involved in a Catholic men's movement called "Answer the Call." The organiza-tion's mission is to rally Catholic

Courtesy of the University of Akron

On the sidelines at the University of Akron

men around the causes of God, family, and the richness of their faith. Central to this movement is a love of the Mass, the Eucharist, the Sacrament of Reconciliation, and the rosary. The movement was launched in Cincinnati, and Faust has spoken there as well as in Detroit, New Orleans, Baltimore, Los Angeles and other cities around the country.

Faust was hesitant when he was first asked to speak. "I don't want to be a hypocrite," he said, at the beginning of one speech. "I'm far from perfect, and I struggle every day. You don't truly know yourself until you examine your handicaps. We all have them. I certainly do."

Faust tells fellow men to knock down the walls, to let yourselves become vulnerable in order to be present to the ones you love. "Don't be afraid to express yourselves, to tell your wives and your children that you love them," he continued in one talk.

Gerry and his wife have three grown children—Gerry, Julie and Stephen. In each of their rooms, the Fausts placed statues, one of the Sacred Heart, another of the Blessed Mother and a third of St. Joseph. Each day, before he goes to work, Gerry places a hand on the head of each of those statues and continues to pray for his three adult children.

Twice a year he writes a letter to each of his children, telling them how much he loves them and how much of a gift they are to him and his wife. He also regularly writes to his wife. He read parts of one letter to a large group of men which probably took more courage than it did to lead Notre Dame into Ann Arbor before 103,000 fans to battle mighty Michigan.

Faust said that Marlene, like most wives, nags him from time-to-time. "Wash your hands. Stay away from the food. You never talk to me. You're never home. It just goes in one ear and out the other," said Faust, getting a laugh from his audience.

His letter avoided superficialities. Instead, it came from the heart and concentrated on the love that he and his wife have for each other. In part it said: "You are a beautiful person within. And without you, I could not live. You did a great job raising our children, and you have always been supportive of me. I have great love for you. God bless you. Thanks for being my friend."

On April 4, 2004, Gerry and Marlene celebrated their fortieth wedding anniversary. The Fausts share a common devotion to the Blessed Mother. In fact, when they were young, both prayed that they would marry the right person. Marlene believes a special novena she made as a youth was instrumental in her ultimately meeting and marrying Gerry.

Faust's coaching career has had peaks and valleys. His family stayed in South Bend when he went to be interviewed for the Akron job. "When I first got the Akron job, I slept on the floor in the coaches' office," he said. "That was a letdown, a lot different than the way things were at Notre Dame."

In his eighteen years as the head coach at Archbishop Moeller High School, his teams compiled an astounding 117-17-2 record. His teams averaged less than one loss a year during his tenure. At one point, Moeller won seventy-two out of seventy-three games. The only loss came on a last second field goal. The football hit an upright and barely tumbled over the crossbar to give the opponents a 13-12 victory.

Through thirty-seven years of coaching football, Faust has no regrets. In fact, every day he nurtures his own golden dream. "It was a privilege to coach and teach young men," said Faust. "I see the sun glittering off Notre Dame's Golden Dome because God has always held my hand. One day, he'll let me know how the walk went. I can take that."

For Faust, mere wins and losses pale in comparison to the people he has met, many of them his former players. He recounted the last time he visited a former player named Ted, who was in a hospital dying from Lou Gerhig's Disease. The former player's son also was present. Ted's nose itched but he was too weak to scratch it. He asked his son if he would do it. Faust reported that immediately he said, "I'll do it," and he leaned over the hospital bed and gently scratched his former player's nose.

"I love you, Ted," Faust said.

"I love you, too, Coach," said his former player.

Two days later, Ted died.

During the late 1980s, Faust and his friend Schneider made a pilgrimage to Fatima, Lourdes and Medugorje. During the twenty-day journey, Faust participated in a Mass every day. At Lourdes, one Mass stands out because he had the chance to meet a special Irishman, a forty-eight year old man battling terminal cancer.

Gerry promised to pray for the man, but he asked Faust to offer his prayers for others, including his sons and especially for the children who had been brought to Lourdes in need of healing. "I have lived my life," the man told Gerry. "I don't need any miracles. God has been good to me. If you say any prayers, say them for these sick children who really need a miracle."

From that day on, Gerry said, "I never prayed that we would win football games again."

At Medugorje, Faust had an opportunity to meet with a visionary to whom it is alleged the Blessed Mother has appeared. Faust's brief conversation with the young woman was translated by an interpreter.

"What should we do when we are repeatedly tempted?" asked Faust.

Faust was given a one-word answer, "Prayer."

What did he learn? "Now I know what has to be done," he said, recalling the brief encounter with the seer.

Faust said that he did not see the sun spin at Medugorje and that he experienced no natural manifestation of God's grace at work in his life, although the same cannot be said of his friend Schneider. Shortly after they returned home, Gerry received a telephone call from Ken. "He told me the color of his rosary had changed from silver to gold," said Faust.

When Gerry told his parents, they immediately asked him why his rosary had not changed color. "I told them I didn't need a miracle," said Faust. "I believed in the apparitions all along."

For years, Faust has prayed the rosary in his car while driving back and forth to work. "I don't listen to the radio," he said. "Those talk shows stink. All they do is beat up on coaches."

As it turned out, Faust forgot about Ken's news that his rosary had changed color. Then, weeks later, while driving to work, he reached for his rosary and was startled to discover that it had changed color, too. Faust laughed when he was asked if the shade of the new color, visible where the beads for the Our Father links the five decades of Hail Marys, was Akron University gold or Notre Dame gold.

Seldom are prayers answered without a new set of trials. Such was the case after the Fausts began a new life at Notre Dame. Moving from Moeller High School to Notre Dame was a difficult time for them, especially for a family whose roots were in the Cincinnati area. "I cried all the way to South Bend," said Marlene.

Incidentally, Marlene's closest friend is Schneider's wife, Janet. Gerry and Ken met through their wives. "Janet and Marlene's friendship goes way back," said Ken. "I think they held hands on their way to kindergarten."

After Notre Dame crushed the Louisiana State University Tigers in Gerry's debut as head coach of the Fighting Irish, Marlene thought to herself, "This is going to be a continuation of the type of success we enjoyed at Moeller."

It did not happen, although adversity drew the family closer. "Gerry got mad at me when I questioned why he was no longer the coach at Notre

Dame," said Marlene. "I got upset at God, too. My husband was an excellent coach, and he exemplified everything that Notre Dame stands for."

Reflecting on his time at Notre Dame, Gerry said. "I was the right man for Notre Dame, if not the right coach."

Win or lose, Gerry Faust has always taken the high road while traveling his personal journey of faith. "There is nothing synthetic about Gerry," said Schneider. "He is genuine, he believes God is guiding him and he is an eternal optimist. The Notre Dame experience was his biggest cross, and he is more of a man because of the way he handles adversity."

At a young age, Gerry was shaped and molded by his father's tough love. His father, Gerard, whose nickname was "Fuzzy," coached and taught at Dayton's Chaminade Catholic High School for fifty-one years. Gerry, a quarterback with modest ability, played football for his father at Chaminade. Following high school, Faust played quarterback for the Dayton University Flyers. His two coaches were Bud Kerr and Hugh Devore, both Notre Dame alumni.

The punishment for mistakes on the football field was severe. Players had to bend over, and Gerry's father applied a belt to their backsides. Gerry felt the sting of that belt more often than anyone else on the team.

"In those days, it was called tough love," said Faust. "Today, they would call it abuse. But my father did it because he was trying to get the team to rally behind me."

"Many days after practice, I never spoke to my father all the way home in the car," said Gerry, who said he never doubted his parents' love for him. "They are the two most saintly people I have ever known."

When both parents were dying, Gerry kept a prayerful vigil at their bedsides and slept on the floor in their hospital rooms. At the funeral Mass for his father, there were sixteen priests on the altar, four of whom were his former players. His mother died November 3, 1991, and his father died on July 6, 1993.

St. Teresa of Avila said that there are more tears shed over answered prayers than unanswered prayers. Certainly, the answer to Faust's prayer to coach Notre Dame brought him and his family stress and heartache. But if one goes through the fire, what comes out is pure gold.

In his years as an assistant vice president for public affairs and development at Akron University, Gerry spoke to more than 80,000 high school students on the importance of ethics and Christian values.

Faust, in all that he does, has made a commitment to be faithful in good times and bad, through victories and defeat.

(This chapter is based primarily on interviews with Gerry Faust and others. Also consulted was The Golden Dream, written by Gerry Faust and Steve Love and published by Sagamore Publishing of Champaign, Illinois.)

Bowie Kuhn
with wife Luisa and grandsons Kyle and Gordie

A Call to Love

From Commissioner of Major League Baseball to itinerant preacher, George "Bowie" Kuhn has experienced many twists and turns while he traveled his personal journey of faith.

Kuhn, a lawyer, cherishes his faith more every day. Today, he addresses men's groups around the country, sharing his faith, his experience and his wisdom.

In May 1998, Kuhn was a featured speaker at the New England Catholic Men's Conference. The Archdiocese of Boston and The Men of St. Joseph were co-sponsors of the event. The Men of St. Joseph, an organization of committed Catholic men, was started in the Diocese of Manchester, New Hampshire. It has gained both a national and international reputation.

Perhaps because it was always clear where he stood, Kuhn has been described as "the last real Commissioner of Baseball." As he spoke to three thousand Catholic men in Lowell, Massachusetts, he was also clear why he had traveled from his home in Ponte Vedra Beach, Florida, to speak in Lowell.

"To put it into one sentence, I am here because I am madly in love with Jesus Christ," Kuhn said. "I surrendered to God long ago."

At six feet four inches, Kuhn is impressive physically as well as spiritually. But on this day, the former commission was reflecting on the life of the man who is said to have been short in stature—St. Paul. He too was accused of being mad.

"You are mad, Paul," Kuhn said, quoting the admonishment of Festus, the ancient Roman governor of Judea. "Much learning is driving you mad." (Acts 26:24)

"They were partly right," said Kuhn of St. Paul's accusers. "It was the 'mad' love for Jesus that dominated Paul and his life."

As a theme, Kuhn selected courage, a virtue vital in the exercise of faith. He said that endurance, willingness to suffer pain, embracing the Cross of Christ—sacrificing for what is morally good and right—are all elements of courage. He also made the distinction between courage and bravery, a worldly trait devoid of transcendent value but championed by many, including author Ernest Hemingway.

Kuhn lamented what he considers a terrible loss, especially for those who profess the Catholic faith. "In today's Catholic world, the crucifix is vanishing because many are captivated by a modernist notion that pain is a totally bad thing," he said. "If that were true, then Christ's crucifixion would be a totally bad thing."

Kuhn also said that instead of hiding from or avoiding pain, followers of Christ must pick up their crosses—which takes courage. "It is not a gentle thing," said Kuhn, about taking up the cross. "But one way or another, everyone is called to Calvary."

In sports, because the platform is so visible and the potential for good is so great, the former baseball commissioner said there should be many more heroes—athletes who stand out because of their personal courage. "There are some," he said. "But what is regrettable, I am afraid, is that there are many more examples of pride and arrogance."

He named several exceptions; athletes he considers heroes. The list included Lou Gehrig, the Iron Man of baseball, who gave his name to amyotrophic lateral sclerosis. Gehrig will always be remembered as a true giant, both on and of the baseball field. Kuhn cited Cal Ripken, the Baltimore Orioles' infielder who broke Gehrig's record of consecutive games played as another baseball hero. Among non-baseball sports figures, he cited figure skater Tara Lipinski and Reggie White, the powerful defensive lineman of the Green Bay Packers.

Kuhn said that the lithe and charmingly youthful Lipinski, an Olympic gold medallist, became a towering sports figure in his eyes when she told a worldwide television audience that "her model and the saint she prays to for intercession is St. Therese of Lisieux."

As for White, an ordained Baptist minister, he was attacked by the media after he spoke the truth which much of society rejects. "The Reverend Reggie White demonstrated tremendous courage," said Kuhn. "He knew he would be attacked and he was. When I look for heroes, I don't look for people who are politically correct; I look for people who are politically incorrect."

In terms of heroes and role models, Kuhn does not have to look far to find his number one hero. In fact, she is right by his side and has been for over four decades. Her name is Luisa, his wife. "I love her," said Kuhn. "And she is my hero."

Kuhn was born on October 2, 1926 in Tacoma Park, Maryland. He is a descendant of two Maryland governors, as well as frontiersman Jim Bowie, who invented the Bowie knife. He attended Franklin and Marshall College, but transferred to Princeton, graduating in 1947. Kuhn enrolled at the University of Virginia Law School and graduated in 1950. He was a practicing attorney, whose duties included representing Major League Baseball and its many interests before he was named commissioner in 1969.

The Kuhns have been blessed with four children and eight grandchildren. The former baseball commissioner told several delightful stories about how he introduces his grandchildren to the wonders and mysteries of God's love." Grandparents have so many marvelous opportunities," he said. Such relationships, said Kuhn, begin in the heart. "Most critical is the open expression of love. That is what God expects in relationships between members of families; fathers, mothers, sons, daughters, grandparents, grandsons, and granddaughters."

Kuhn shared much about himself and his life as a disciple of Christ. He said he was born in 1926 on the feast of St. Jude, the patron saint of lost causes, during the presidency of Calvin Coolidge, whom he said was "a good, estimable man historians have elected to keep hidden from us."

About the patronage of St. Jude, he said: "St. Jude has gotten me through my own dark days."

He said he has a guardian angle named "Tom" in honor of Thomas Merton. Merton's *Seven Story Mountain*, a book he read years ago, rejuvenated his spiritual life. Within the past few years, the Kuhns made a pilgrimage to the Holy Land, which Bowie said was life-changing. "I am a different person today after having gone to the Holy Land."

During his post-baseball life, the former baseball commissioner has been inspired by little people; the sick, the lame, the forgotten whom much of the world ignores. Two such people, he referred to simply as "Mary and Jimmy."

Mary, an African-American woman, was a terminally ill AIDS patient at an acute-care hospital in New York where Kuhn volunteered, after being "pushed" to do so by Cardinal John O'Connor, the Archbishop of New York. "She had a beautiful smile," said Kuhn. "And I was totally in love with her."

During his visits, Kuhn hugged her and the two prayed. "I read the Bible and she followed along," he said. She was proud of her children and she showed the former baseball commissioner photographs of them. "Mary was totally blind," said Kuhn. "She thought of her children as being beautiful, but she had only seen them through the eyes of her mind."

One day, Kuhn returned to the hospital and discovered that Mary's room was empty. After checking with the main desk of the ward, he learned that the inevitable had happened. Mary had been called home to God.

As for Jimmy, a second friend who is very much alive, the two men met on a pilgrimage to Lourdes. Jimmy has cerebral palsy which limits his physical capabilities, yet at the same time allows his soul to soar. Through the gift of faith, Jimmy believes all things are possible. During Pope John Paul II's visit to Denver for World Youth Day, Jimmy was one of the speakers. He was supposed to speak for only five minutes. Undaunted, Jimmy spoke for

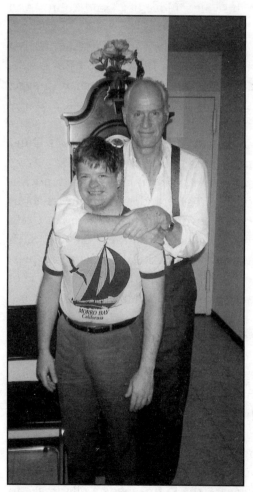

Courtesy of Bowie Kuhn

Bowie and Jimmy

twelve minutes. At the conclusion of his talk, the Holy Father, with tears streaming down his cheeks, beckoned Jimmy to come to him. Jimmy and the Pope embraced and the photograph of that heart-warming scene was published in newspapers across the country and the world.

Today, Jimmy is a Eucharistic Minister at St. Stephen of Hungary Church in New York City. Before giving Eucharist to others, Jimmy is permitted to make a statement. Here is what he says: "Before I give out the body of Christ, I have something to say. My name is Jimmy and the priests have honored me with the gift of being a Eucharistic Minister. I have cerebral palsy. Sometimes I stumble when I walk down stairs and I have to hold on to the altar. Please do not be afraid of me. I want to give you Jesus Christ."

But back to baseball. Bowie Kuhn was named the Commissioner of Major League Baseball in 1969 and held the position for sixteen years. During that time, the game prospered. First and foremost, he considered himself a guardian of the national pastime—truly America's game. "We tried to take the game to morally higher ground," he said. "And I believe the game is better because of that effort."

As commissioner, he said, "I may have let an owner down here, a player or a sports writer down there, but I tried never to let down my Lord."

The men he spoke to in Lowell come from an area known euphemistically as Red Sox Nation. Kuhn told the men how thrilled he was the first time he visited Fenway Park for the 1967 World Series. As for the New York Yankees, Boston's bitter rivals, he said: "If there are any Yankee fans in the audience, they had best follow the example of St. Joseph and keep quiet."

He also broke startling new ground when he said, in jest, that there actually are eleven, not ten Commandments. "The eleventh Commandment is: Thou Shalt Not Tear Down Fenway Park." It was a remark that brought the house down.

George Bowie Kuhn is both a man of courage and a man of faith, personal strengths that will outlive all things temporal, even baseball.

Jim Lonborg

The Glory Never Fades

James Reynold Lonborg has lived through many shining moments, both on and off baseball fields. The ex-big league pitcher hurled the Boston Red Sox to an "Impossible Dream" pennant in 1967, and in the process, pocketed the coveted Cy Young Award for being the top pitcher in the American League.

However, the brightest moment of Lonborg's life had nothing to do with fleeting athletic fame, but everything to do with the partnership and commitment embodied in the Sacrament of Marriage.

"The day that I met Rosemary was the most important day of my life," said Lonborg. "And meeting her was the single greatest thing that has ever happened to me."

The couple met in 1970, at a singles club where Rosemary worked as a hostess. They married the next year, 1971, his final season with the Red Sox. The Lonborgs have been blessed with six children, three of their own and three adopted children, including a Korean son and a Korean daughter.

After adopting their first child, the Lonborgs adopted two Korean youngsters. Then, nine months after the arrival of the Asian children, Rosemary gave birth to her first child. At the time, Jim pitched for the

Philadelphia Phillies. On the night of Nora's birth, Lonborg celebrated the blessed occasion by hurling a one-hit shutout against the Cincinnati Reds at Veterans Stadium in Philadelphia.

During his fourteen-year career in the major leagues, Lonborg pitched for three teams—the Red Sox, the Phillies and the Milwaukee Brewers. The handsome 6-foot-5 right-hander won 157 games. Bob Boone, Russ Gibson, Mike Ryan and the late Elston Howard were four of the outstanding defen-

National Baseball Hall of Fame Library, Cooperstown, NY

1967 World Series

Lonborg delivers the first pitch of the game at Fenway Park against the St. Louis Cardinals.

sive catchers who caught Big Jim's zipping fastballs and sharp-breaking curves and sliders.

Over the years, Jim and Rosemary have formed a team where family values are nurtured based on the indissolubility and primacy of the marriage sacrament.

"Everything in our family is based on our relationship," said Lonborg. "The stability of our family life stems from the intense friendship we share and the deep love that Rosemary and I have for each other. The children not only see that, but they also experience it as well."

Others who know the Lonborgs recognize the strength of Jim and Rosemary's marriage. Lonborg, a Stanford University graduate, was nicknamed "Gentleman Jim" during his baseball career.

"It is a perfect description of the man," said Msgr. Eugene P. McNamara, pastor of St. Mary of the Nativity Parish in Scituate, Massachusetts, where the Lonborgs are parishioners. "When Jim and Rosemary are together, you can feel the love that exists between them."

As part of their community involvement, the Lonborgs chaperone monthly dances for junior high and high school students. Most youngsters would feel awkward if their parents were the supervising adults at such social events; not the Lonborg children.

> Everything in our family is based on our relationship," said Lonborg. "The stability of our family life stems from the intense friendship we share and the deep love that Rosemary and I have for each other. The children not only see that, but they also experience it as well."

"Jim and Rosemary's children have more than just respect for their parents," explained Msgr. McNamara. "They idolize Jim, they love Rosemary, and they are very proud to have both of them attend their social events."

Jim credits Rosemary for any success they share in their roles as parents. "Jim is a very humble man," said Msgr. McNamara. "He always gives credit for all his blessings to Rosemary."

When Msgr. McNamara reflects on the Lonborg's marriage he is reminded of the poignant admonition to the bride and groom, part of the

Catholic marriage ceremony included in the pre-Vatican II Roman rite: "sacrifice is usually difficult and irksome. Only love can make it easy and perfect love can make it a joy."

As a youth, Lonborg was raised in the Episcopal faith, but he converted to Catholicism because of Rosemary's example and his own desire to share a closer spiritual union with his wife and children. "Rosemary is the one who always had great faith," he said. "My faith has grown through her and the children. For years, I went to Mass with them and I always felt comfortable."

Father Thomas Gillespie, another Greater Boston area priest, guided Lonborg through the Rite of Christian Initiation of Adults program. At the time that Jim was a catechumen, Father Gillespie said he was struck by the wonder of God's grace building on nature and expressed in the person of Jim Lonborg.

"Jim is what you see," said Father Gillespie. "He is genuinely that nice of a guy. Decency seeks to express itself, and the Catholic faith is a spiritual vehicle that allows Jim, through his wonderful human nature, to be the type of person God created him to become."

For as far back as he can remember, Lonborg has always sought God. Once he told Father Gillespie that when he was flying from city to city during his big-league baseball career, he often leaned back in his airplane seat and felt very close to God. When Jim and Rosemary met, she immediately detected his strength of character, although she said she was unimpressed by the fact that he was a ballplayer.

"I felt sorry for him after I found out he was a baseball player," she said. "I always thought you did something like that when you couldn't do anything else."

However, once Rosemary overcame her prejudice against professional athletes, she discovered that she had met a gem of a man. "Everything about Jim amazed me," she said. "He had so much going for him on the outside, and he was so gentle, kind and good on the inside."

Father Gillespie said that the Lonborgs are examples of oneness in marriage. "When you speak with Jim and Rosemary it is like talking to one person. They are truly two joined as one in Christ."

When Jim started to plan his life after baseball, Rosemary helped him make the decision to attend dental school. "We talked about it during a weekend in Vermont," said Lonborg.

Today, Lonborg is a dentist with a thriving practice in Hanover, Massachusetts. After he decided to return to school, the family had to make financial sacrifices. As a baseball player, Lonborg never was paid the astronomical amount of money the professional athletes command today. One Christmas season, Rosemary even worked as a waitress so the family could afford to splurge on gifts.

As a boy, Lonborg grew up in San Luis Obispo, California. It is part of Big Sur Country, through which Highways 1 and 101 wind, halfway between Los Angeles and San Francisco. The area is famed for its spectacular natural beauty. "Naturally speaking, it is about as close to heaven on earth as you can get," said Lonborg, who as a youth, spent time hiking, hunting and swimming.

Courtesy of Jim Lonborg

The Lonborg family
Back Row (from left): Jim, Claire, Phoebe, Nora, and Rosemary.
Front row: Jordan, Nicky, and John.

Father Gillespie believes that the young Lonborg gained inner strength while communing with nature.

"In his own way, he has always been a contemplative," said Father Gillespie. "When he ventured into those California hills he was praying without being conscious of it."

Lonborg's youth, however, was not always filled by sunshine. Reality had its share of darkness. When he was fifteen, his parents divorced. Lonborg said the divorce was particularly traumatic for him and his brother and sister. Despite his own pain, he never became bitter.

"Once the pitch is out of the pitcher's hand, there is nothing you can do about it," said Lonborg. "You can't take it back. Instead of becoming resentful, I thought about the good times from the past and then concentrated on the present and the future."

He also learned the importance of discipline at an early age. "Young people have to cultivate the habit of saying no to their impulses and desires," said Jim, who is far from a prude and enjoyed life when he was a bachelor and a gifted professional athlete.

The ability to discipline oneself, Father Gillespie pointed out, is the beginning of discernment. "A man as prominent as Jim Lonborg has a thousand distractions." said Father Gillespie. "Jim doesn't allow himself to get distracted because prayer has taught him wisdom."

Lonborg still glows from the memory of the Summer of 1967. His 22-9 record was a major factor in the Red Sox successful pennant drive. Another major factor was the superlative play of Hall of Fame member Carl Yastrzemski, who won the triple crown and was named Most Valuable Player. "That season was so special," Lonborg said. "The baseball excitement influenced all areas of my life and gave me a sense that I wanted to stay in New England." That season also revived the Boston franchise and restored interest in baseball throughout New England.

Lonborg won two games in the 1967 World Series. But Bob Gibson, the most dominant right-handed pitcher of his era, won three games in the Series. The St. Louis Cardinals captured the series by winning the seventh and deciding game.

In the 1967 World Series, Lonborg pitched a brilliant one-hit shutout and a sparkling three-hitter. Neither was his best performance, however. Lonborg said the best pitch he ever made was the day he asked Rosemary to marry him.

Today, faith and family anchor the Lonborgs' life. In 1991, Jim and Rosemary served as chairpersons of the Archdiocese of Boston's annual Cardinal's Appeal fund raising drive.

Rosemary uses the word "roundness" to describe the life of her family. She has even written and published a book for children based on the strength of a quiet father, husband, lay Catholic, citizen, dentist, and ex-big leaguer named Dr. Jim Lonborg, D.M.D.

Rear Admiral Thomas Lynch

The Shipmate

As the 54th Superintendent of the United States Naval Academy and a career Navy officer with over thirty years of service, Rear Admiral Thomas C. Lynch might not have sea water in his veins, but his personal resolve and dedication to duty would rival that of Ernest Hemingway's bloody but unbowed fisherman in the novel *The Old Man and the Sea*.

Admiral Lynch, choose three unambiguous words—ship, shipmate and self—to outline a specific code of ethics or moral mandate that defines all that it means to be a midshipman at Annapolis. It is a philosophy at odds with contemporary, selfish attitudes so widespread throughout society because it challenges individuals to place others ahead of themselves.

"We teach the Brigade of Midshipmen, in word and deed, to always consider the effects of leadership on my ship and my shipmate," said Admiral Lynch.

At Annapolis, individual self-sacrifice is ingrained in all that the U.S. Navy stands for, according to the admiral. "As a midshipman, I must learn humility. That means putting myself last while demonstrating concern for my fellows, my ship and my mission. Without that quality, that type of personal character, I will not succeed," he said.

Admiral Lynch draws a parallel between the ideals of the Naval Academy and an elementary tenet of Christian faith: loving your neighbor as you love your self. "It is a saintly goal and it challenges the individual in the true Christian and Catholic sense," Lynch said

As superintendent, Admiral Lynch was a guardian of the Naval Academy's tradition of molding military leaders who are committed to service and duty. "I would say my most important task was to make it possible for everyone at Annapolis, from the Commandant of Midshipmen to the cooks in the dining room, to do their jobs," he said.

For everyone, the environment can be either a help or a hindrance in pursuit of that end. At Annapolis, Admiral Lynch attempted to guarantee that a distinct "Navy Blue and Gold" climate enhanced the navigation of a shared mission.

Admiral Lynch's values took root at home. As the second oldest of five children, he learned the importance of common denominators at an early age. He grew up in Lima, Ohio. His dad was actually the first superintendent in the Lynch family. "My father was Superintendent of the Western Ohio Gas Company," he reported.

Courtesy of the United States Naval Academy

Midshipman Lynch

As a youth, he was an altar boy, and he was molded by two religious orders, the Dominicans and the Sisters of Charity. He characterized his parents as "positive examples of all that it means to live a Christian life." His father taught him his own personal motto to live by: "Work with all your might. Pray with all your heart and soul. Leave the rest to God. Don't worry and don't have any regrets, because what does not work out is not God's will anyway!"

At age thirteen, a *Life* Magazine cover story changed the direction of his life, although he altered the script slightly. It was a 1958 spread featuring Pete Dawkins—Captain of the West Point Corps of Cadets, Captain of the

Army football team, All-American, Heisman Trophy winner and Rhodes Scholar.

"After reading that story, I knew exactly what I wanted to do with my life," said Admiral Lynch.

However, somewhere along the way of conceptualizing a dream and shaping it into reality, the Army march "The Caissons Go Rolling Along" hit a beach and the musical beat ringing in his ears switched to the high seas and the Navy theme "Anchors Aweigh."

Admiral Lynch salutes West Point with heartfelt respect, but he ended up at Annapolis. Go Navy. Beat Army. The Navy goat versus the Army mule. "I knew an engineer who was a Naval Academy graduate," he said. "I didn't know a congressman, but the right connection was made and nine months later I was headed to Annapolis. It is just one more example of the Lord taking care of me."

Admiral Lynch graduated with academic and leadership distinction in the U. S. Naval Academy Class of 1964. He also was a center, linebacker and captain of the Navy football team, Coach Wayne Hardin's 9-2 Middies, a club that posted a terrific season but lost to the Texas Longhorns in the 1964 Cotton Bowl, 28-6.

Roger Staubach, quarterback, Heisman Trophy winner and pro football Hall of Famer, was Admiral Lynch's friend and teammate.

Father Joseph Ryan, a former Annapolis Catholic chaplain, remembered that Lynch was such a rugged individual that, in addition to his football prowess, he was the Naval Academy's heavyweight boxing champion.

With the heavyweight crown on the line, Dick Merritt, a

Courtesy of the United States Naval Academy

At the Naval Academy

tackle on the Navy football team, and Lynch staged a bloody brawl for the title. Both were brutes who weighed around two hundred and thirty pounds. "They were good friends," said Father Ryan, "but they fought like they hated each other. They were big, strong guys and they put on fierce, toe-to-toe battles."

Admiral Lynch, whose younger brother, Jim, captained the Notre Dame football team and later was a linebacker for the Kansas City Chiefs, believes that many of the lessons he learned from athletics are applicable to life.

"Athletics teach you the importance of self-sacrifice, determination and resiliency," he said. "When I missed a block, I had to drag my butt off the ground, forget about it and try even harder on the next play. Football is a lot like life. There are a lot of ups and downs, bumps and bruises."

Sometimes there is exhilaration, too—like being captain of a Navy football team that beat Army for the fifth straight season and walloped Notre Dame, 34-14, in October of 1963 at Notre Dame Stadium, the last time the Middies defeated the Fighting Irish.

Edward "Skip" Orr was a wide receiver and defensive back on the 1963 Navy football team and is now an account manager for The Staubach Company, former teammate Roger Staubach's thriving real estate business. Lynch and Orr remain close friends. Orr believes that the Admiral's impact on family life, his own and others, is his crowning achievement. "The proof of the pudding about Tom Lynch is reflected by his family," said Orr. "He and his wife have three great kids. They are personable, bright and they have character. They grew up in the military, and obviously the principles that Tom stands for have rubbed off on them."

Father Ryan, a friend of the family, who officiated at the marriage of the Admiral's daughter, Jill, characterizes Admiral Lynch as someone who possesses the zeal of Saint Ignatius of Loyola and who works for the forces of good against the powers of darkness. "He is a man of quiet strength," said Father Ryan. "Tom is not flamboyant, but his faith is deep and sincere. He leads by example."

Just as gold is purified by fire, leadership is sharpened by the sting of trial and difficulty. During his tenure as Superintendent of the Naval Academy (1991-94), Admiral Lynch faced many problems, including a reduction of forces and resources, reports of declining morale in every branch of the military, a congressional investigation into a cheating scandal that challenged the Honor Code and resulted in the expulsion of twenty-four midshipmen, and the controversial acceptance of gays in the military.

On the question of homosexuals in the military, Admiral Lynch said this: "Each of us, whether we are civilians or in the military, has our own personal views on the subject of homosexuality. In the final analysis, the American people, through their elected officials, will decide what is right and just."

Admiral Lynch does not believe, however, that the issue of homosexual rights is comparable to the progress that has been made in race relations. "It is not the same thing as civil rights," he said. "I agree with General [Colin] Powell on the subject. He points out that race is a benign characteristic, but homosexuality is a behavioral characteristic."

As a career military officer, Admiral Lynch would never publicly criticize his Commander and Chief, President Clinton, who advocated lifting the ban on homosexuals entering the military, but eventually agreed to a compromise, even if he disagreed with him on a particular issue.

The chain of command in the military is similar to the hierarchical tier of authority in religious life where superiors, like bishops, expect fidelity from their subordinates. However, the fine line between freedom of conscience and obedience out of respect for duty has been the subject of debate for ages.

"You have to remember," said Father Robert Doherty, S.J. a professor at Pope John XXIII National Seminary in Weston, Massachusetts, "that an ethical military code is not a religious vow. Everyone is subject to his or her own individual conscience in matters of right and wrong. Sometimes you remain silent when you disagree and other times you have to speak out. Only the individual can decide what constitutes the greater good."

For many, the transition from civilian to military life is traumatic. Individualism has no place in the military. Adjusting to the military can even be a shock, says Orr, an Annapolis graduate and a former Navy officer. "The military is not a democracy," he said. "There is no room for questioning a superior's order. Many young people respond well to the military way of doing things. But the transition is difficult and painful, particularly at the beginning."

Obedience often means doing something unpleasant or something a person does not like. It is not easy and everyone is confronted by the challenge. "I'll bet Colin Powell (the former chairman of the Joints Chief of Staff), knowing that President Clinton is not a veteran, found it difficult to introduce him at the Vietnam Memorial," said Orr. "But he did it out of duty and respect for the Office of Commander-in-Chief."

Respect is the touchstone of interpersonal relations in the military. It is the lifeblood of day-to-day existence, the filial bond that unites every soldier, sailor and marine, says Lynch. "If I am going to follow you into battle, I must trust you, have confidence in you, and I must respect you."

The Admiral also said that there is no place in the military for anything that undermines the faith one has in another member of the armed forces.

During his years as Superintendent, the Admiral and his wife, Kathleen, were hosts to thousands of guests, including former British Prime Minister Margaret Thatcher.

> Respect is the touchstone of interpersonal relations in the military. It is the lifeblood of day-to-day existence, the filial bond that unites every soldier, sailor and marine, says Lynch. "If I am going to follow you into battle, I must trust you, have confidence in you, and I must respect you."

"At Annapolis, we shared everything," said Admiral Lynch. "Even our home."

During his Navy career, Admiral Lynch served as Navy Chief of Legislative Affairs and was Commander of the Cruiser-Destroyer Group Twelve, the first battle group on the scene in the Red Sea after the Iraq invasion of Kuwait.

He looks to the future with confidence and faith. "There are always going to be Saadam Husseins in the world," he said. "But we have the finest young people in the world answering the call to duty. Just looking around Annapolis, I am not concerned about the future of the United States of America."

Over the years, that great Navy Cotton Bowl team of 1963 has been reunited on several occasions. Almost everyone attends the reunions. It was a team that had chemistry, that bonded, and got the most out of its collective abilities. "Every time we get together, the spirit is still there," said both Admiral Lynch and his former teammate Orr. "You can feel it."

Recently, rumors have circulated about the prospects of Staubach, the most celebrated athlete on the 1963 Navy team, running for public office. Admiral Lynch wholeheartedly endorses the idea. "Roger Staubach is the finest human being I have ever met," he said. "Whether it is as mayor, city councilor, governor, senator, congressman or President, our country needs Roger's high standards, his faith, his hope for the future, his moral values, his common sense, his clear thinking and his proven record of solving problems and getting things done. I have encouraged Roger to pursue government service. I believe it is in his bones."

National Baseball Hall of Fame Library, Cooperstown, NY

Mickey Mantle

Number 7

If Dwight David Eisenhower, the thirty-fourth president of the United States, was the most popular American during the 1950s, Mickey Charles Mantle was clearly number two on the hit parade.

It is impossible to think about the 1950s and not call to mind the two men, different though they were.

Mickey Mantle defined the sports' landscape during post-World War II America. You need not even mention his name, just the number 7 evoked thoughts of the future Hall of Famer.

Mantle was a blond, blue-eyed Oklahoman with a boyish grin. He was bigger than life—like a mythical figure, chiseled in granite, who had suddenly turned into flesh and blood. He could run from home plate to first base in the blazingly fast time of 3.1 seconds. He was a switch-hitter blessed with prodigious power from either side of the plate, and when he took over center field for the New York Yankees, he replaced an American icon named Joe DiMaggio.

The first time I saw him play was at Boston's Fenway Park, during the early 1950s in a game against the Red Sox. We got there early, as soon as the gates opened, to watch the Yankees take batting practice. With a scorecard in one hand and a hot dog in the other, my eyes immediately searched for Mickey Mantle.

Once I spotted him, I never took my eyes off number 7. I followed him as he moved into and out of the dugout. I watched him swinging two or three bats as he prepared to hit. I literally gasped as he stepped into the batting cage and began unloading one blast after another to the deepest parts of the park and beyond.

On his last swing, he laid down a drag bunt, another of his trademark talents. As the ball trickled down the first base line in fair territory, Mantle had exploded out of the left-hand batter's box, carrying his bat with him. His movements were smooth and effortless, and he bunted and ran in one fluid, extended motion. He was the picture of grace and power. I continued to watch him as he stretched, played catch, joked with teammates, signed an occasional autograph, and jogged to the outfield.

At the time, I was a Boston Braves' fan, and when Boston's National League team moved to Milwaukee in 1953, I felt jilted. The Braves' Sam Jethroe was the first African-American to play major league baseball for a Boston team, and he was my favorite center fielder. As a rookie in 1950, he hit eighteen home runs for the Braves and took National League Rookie of the Year honors. In his freshman season, he clouted eighteen home runs and stole thirty-five bases.

Jethroe, who could fly around the bases and had plenty of pop in his bat, was an erratic fielder. In fact, on several occasions, I saw him almost get "skulled" on routine high-fly balls hit to center field. Like so many African-American ball players of that era, he was no spring chicken when he finally made it to the big leagues. He starred for years in the Negro Leagues before catching on with the Braves. He played three seasons for the Braves and one season with the Pittsburgh Pirates. By 1954, his big league career was over. The last I heard, he owned Jethroe's Steak House in Pittsburgh. I spoke to him there once while researching a story on the old Braves.

After the Braves moved to Milwaukee in 1953, the Red Sox, sadly, was the only game in town. So while Mantle played center field for the Yankees two hundred miles away in New York, I had to be satisfied watching players such as Jimmy Piersall, Tom Umphlett, Gary Geiger, Willie Tasby, Lenny Green and Don Demeter play center field for the Red Sox.

As great a fielder as Piersall was, he was no Mantle. And as for the others, well, is it any wonder Red Sox fans developed an inferiority complex over the group of also-rans in center field? Look at who New York City had during those years—Mantle, Willie Mays (Giants) and Duke Snyder (Dodgers). In New York, they argued about who was the best of the three; in Boston they just argued.

Shortly before Mantle died and long after he had stopped wearing the pin stripes and gray baseball flannels for the Yankees, Mickey Mantle became a Page One story again.

By the time Mantle turned sixty-three years old, it took a liver transplant to save his life. Even that was just for a short time. There were a lot of people who thought that the liver should have gone to someone more deserving than a sports celebrity who drowned his major organs in an ocean of beer and hard liquor.

Maybe they were right.

No one ever said life was fair.

Perhaps they felt, with justification, that Mantle was just another spoiled and fatally flawed sports hero who never grew up while he played and remained shamefully irresponsible long after his Hall of Fame career ended.

They may have been right about that, too. Mantle never claimed to be a model husband, father, citizen, or even a sober adult for that matter.

He died on August 13, 1995, succumbing to the ravages of cancer.

But he went out like a champion.

Before he died, he dried out, abstained from all forms of alcoholic beverages and apologized for his sins to God, to his wife and children and to the countless youths who idolized him.

He not only sought their forgiveness, he spent his final days making amends to them and imploring others to learn from the mistakes he had made.

And in the end, Mantle found peace.

His personal conversion allowed the grace of God to change his heart and was the most important act of his life. It was bigger than any thing else he ever did, and that includes the moon shot he blasted off Camilo Pascual of the Washington Senators which came within a whisker of being the only ball anyone has ever hit completely out of Yankee Stadium.

As a ball player, he was a product of phenomenal natural ability, plus a strong parental influence. His father, Mutt, taught him to switch hit in the early evening after spending long, sooty days working in the Northern Oklahoma mines.

By making it to the big leagues, Mickey fulfilled his father's dream of seeing his son play for the Yankees. The elder Mantle died, also of cancer, at the age of forty-one, soon after watching twenty year old Mickey play in the 1951 World Series against the New York Giants.

Mantle had an uncle who also died at an early age and that left Mickey

Courtesy of the New York Yankees

Don't Kick!

June 12, 1951: Looks as if New York Yankees Mickey Mantle is at the hard end of a swift kick by St. Louis Browns shortstop John Bero, but Bero's trying to get out of the New Yorker's way after fielding Phil Rizzuto's grounder. Backing up the play is Browns second baseman Bob Young.

with a fixation about death. For years, Mantle felt certain that, like his father and uncle, he would die at a young age. That might explain why he played so hard and partied so zealously.

"I always regretted that I didn't take better care of my body," Mantle remarked years after his great career was over.

Injuries tormented him during his entire career. In the 1951 World Series, he got his spikes caught in an outfield water drain and tore up a knee. His bones were brittle, a consequence of osteomyelitis—an inflammation of the bone and bone marrow—a condition that developed after he was kicked playing high school football.

But his powerful body masked his susceptibility to injury and his physical problems. Fans would have been stunned to see Mantle in the pre-game dressing room. By the time the trainers finished wrapping his legs, arms, shoulders, chest and ribs, he looked like a half-dressed mummy. One can only wonder how good he could have become if he had played injury-free.

As a boy, he dreamed about playing halfback for the University of Oklahoma Sooners, but instead signed with the Yankees after scout Tom Greenwade spotted him and offered him a modest $1,500 bonus. That does not seem like much now, but to a family struggling to get by on a miner's income, it was a huge windfall. The bonus was too rich to pass up, no matter how much he wanted to play college football for Coach Bud Wilkinson's Sooners.

As a rookie with the Bronx Bombers, he roomed with a former U.S. Marine, the worldly-wise and street-tough Hank Bauer, who taught the country bumpkin Mantle how to walk, talk and dress like a big leaguer.

Later, he also roomed with two more city slickers, Whitey Ford and Billy Martin. Much to the chagrin of Casey Stengel, the legendary Yankee manager, Mantle and his friends frequented many more nightclubs and barrooms than they did churches, movie houses and museums. In fact, an incident at New York's Copacabana Nightclub drew headlines and resulted in Mantle's buddy, the brash Martin, being traded to the Kansas City A's in 1957.

Yankee management blamed Martin, the scrappy but tempestuous second baseman, for the brawl at the New York nightclub and for other off-the-field problems. Martin was targeted as the ringleader, and a bad influence on other players like Mantle. So the feisty but expendable Martin was shipped to Kansas City, a franchise which the Yankees used like a farm club during that era with a series of trades that beefed up the Yankees' roster for another successful push toward the American League pennant.

Martin might have been the instigator and the fall guy, but Mantle and the others were no angels. Mantle's late night activities sapped his strength and diminished his tremendous talent.

In 1956, Mantle won the MVP and the triple crown with fifty-two home runs, a sizzling .353 batting average and 130 RBIs along with a gaudy .705 slugging percentage. He clouted 536 home runs in eighteen big league seasons, finishing with a .298 career batting average, which haunted him during retirement. As much as anything else, he wanted to complete his career with a .300 or better batting average, but he hung around two seasons too many, hitting .245 in 1967 and .237 in 1968, his final season. If he had not played those final two seasons, or if he had been in better physical shape, he might have hit .305 or better for his career. He set numerous World Series records, including the most home runs with eighteen. He played on twelve pennant winners and seven world champions. Mantle was voted into the Baseball Hall of Fame in 1974.

Until 1998, when Mark McGwire of the St. Louis Cardinals and Sammy Sosa of the Chicago Cubs both broke the single-season record for home runs (McGuire with seventy and Sosa with sixty-six), the 1961 season stood out as the most memorable baseball season of the second half of the century. In that season Mickey Mantle and Roger Maris, both Yankees, staged an unforgettable assault on Babe Ruth's single-season home run record of sixty, a record that had stood for thirty-four years and was thought to be unbreakable.

The chase to overtake The Babe, perhaps the greatest baseball player and most colorful sports figure who has ever lived, captured the imagination of the entire country. By the end of July, Maris, number 9, belted forty homers, and Mantle, number 7, socked thirty-nine. By September 10, Maris' total swelled to fifty-six, and Mantle had fifty-three.

A neck injury, however, forced the crowned prince of New York, Mantle, out of the lineup down the stretch and no one will ever know how frustrated he must have been having to settle for fifty-four homers, finishing second fiddle to Maris. Maris was clearly the underdog, and few wanted to see him break Ruth's record. A Catholic and a deeply spiritual man, he persevered and broke the record on the final day of the regular season when he hit his sixty-first home run off of Tracey Stallard of the Red Sox at Yankee Stadium.

Maris was a shy, reticent North Dakotan who was uncomfortable in the spotlight. The pressure of the home run chase pushed him to the brink of a breakdown and caused his hair to fall out. In contrast to Mantle, he was a good family man and a loner off the field. He also hated talking to the press and resented the intrusion of the media into his life.

It was Mantle, the hard-drinking, carousing superstar, who was the darling of the adoring sports public and the media. After all, he was a true Yankee, who came to the big leagues through the New York system and

Courtesy of the New York Yankees

Mantle is greeted at home plate after one of his 536 home runs.

played his entire career with the Yankees. Even Mantle's teammates, rooted for Mickey, not Roger, to break the Babe's record.

Earlier during his career, Maris played for the Cleveland Indians and later for the Kansas City A's, before being traded to the Yankees prior to the 1960 season. Maris played twelve years in the big leagues, finishing his career on a pennant winner, the 1968 St. Louis Cardinals. He ended up with 275 homers and a mediocre .260 lifetime batting average.

In 1961, when he hit 61 homers, Maris batted .269, and old-timers all across the country raged over the fact that a .269 hitter had the audacity to break the mighty Babe's record. Ruth, they were quick to tell everyone, was a complete ball player, and his lifetime batting average was a robust .342.

Maris was no Ruth, and he certainly was not as good a player as Mantle, either. But I remember sitting in the right field stands at Fenway Park and watching Maris play right field for both the Indians and the A's. I distinctly remember that Maris was a line-drive hitter with a sweet, compact swing. He also was a superb outfielder with a terrific throwing arm. I admired Maris from the first time I saw him play. During the two seasons prior to being traded to the Yankees, Maris hit 44 home runs and drove in 152 runs. I was not surprised by the power he demonstrated after he became a Yankee.

During the 1961 baseball season, it was Maris, to the surprise of all, not Mantle, who became the more notable figure, while Mantle had to settle for a supporting role.

Like Mantle, Maris died from cancer. One can only wonder if stress, particularly during his epic chase of Ruth's record, had weakened his immune system and made him more susceptible to the fatal disease. Roger died on December 14, 1985. He was fifty-one.

In the final analysis, Mickey Mantle was one of the greatest players I ever saw play the game—despite his shortcomings. In fact, he and Willie Mays were the best pair I ever saw play, with Stan Musial and Jackie Robinson also in the top four. Ted Williams, of course, was by far the greatest hitter of the era. But many forget that Williams, at best, was an average outfielder, a lead-footed base runner and hardly a great team player. Willie Mays, for one, was a far superior all-around player than Williams. As were Hank Aaron and Musial, just to name a few.

During the Fabulous 1950s, many folks liked Ike but the sports world was in awe of Mickey Mantle. His incredible talent was diminished by his lifestyle. But in the end, Mickey Mantle proved to be more than just a great ball player. He was a man who admitted he had been wrong. He faced himself and his past life and tried to atone for his mistakes, and with the help of God, he faced the abyss without blinking. With that, he became a model, not just for sports fans, but for us all.

Joe Morgan

The Long Journey

Former Boston Red Sox manager Joe Morgan learned a lesson about being in the right position when he was in the fifth grade and serving as an altar boy at Blessed Sacrament Church in Walpole, Massachusetts.

"We had a ton of altar boys in those days," said Morgan, remembering that in 1941 he and his two brothers were altar boys. "When we lined up for the Stations of the Cross, we had so many altar boys that when the priest was at the first station, there were altar boys as far away as the eighth station."

Unlike the ageless ritual of boys determining who picks first for a sandlot baseball game by grabbing the handle of a bat, there was nothing democratic back then about the process of becoming an altar boy. The pastor, the late Father Bennett Joseph O'Brien, spotted Morgan and ordered him "to go over there to the rack where the cassocks are hanging and pick out one that fits."

"That is how I became an altar boy," Morgan recalled.

Not really. What Morgan described was the mechanics of picking out the proper liturgical dress to respectfully serve Mass. It was the example of a good priest like Father O'Brien that inspired Morgan to become an altar boy. "We looked up to him," said the ex-Red Sox skipper. "He was stern, but he was always fair."

As a big league manager, Morgan was an authoritative figure, too, but he also was known for his congeniality as well as his down-to-earth manner and sense of humor.

After the Red Sox fired John McNamara, Morgan was appointed interim manager on July 14, 1988. At the time, Boston was mired in fourth place in the American League East with a 43-42 record, nine games behind the first place Detroit Tigers. But not for long.

The change of managers did wonders for the Red Sox. With Joe at the controls, the team went on a tear, sweeping an eleven game homestand, winning twelve straight games and capturing nineteen of the first twenty games that Morgan managed the ball club. On July 20, Morgan was appointed the team's permanent manager and on August 3 his contract was extended.

Morgan managed the Red Sox from 1988-91. During that span, the BoSox won two American League East Championships, and Morgan compiled a 305-258 record, finishing with a solid .542 winning percentage.

Joe was born on November 30, 1930. As he looks toward his seventies, he is still a private man. He lives his Catholic faith, just as he always has, quietly but purposively. When he managed the Red Sox and the team played at Fenway Park, Morgan and his wife, Dot, participated in the 7:30 Sunday morning Mass at Blessed Sacrament Church.

Morgan is the second oldest of five children. His father, William, a boiler-room engineer, and his mother, Mary Kennedy Morgan, passed their Catholic faith on to him and his siblings.

"Your faith comes from your family," Morgan said. "I am the same now as I was years ago. My faith has always been there. I am not a religious fanatic. I go to church because I want to."

Morgan's baseball travels parallel a Christian's pilgrim journey of faith. He spent thirty years beating the bushes of the minor leagues as a player, coach, scout and manager. He was a utility player who only played eighty-eight games in the big leagues with five teams—the Milwaukee Braves, the Kansas City Athletics, the Philadelphia Phillies, the Cleveland Indians, and the St. Louis Cardinals.

Before coming to the Red Sox as a coach in 1985, Morgan managed in the minor leagues for sixteen seasons. There is no mystery of why he shook the dust of minor league stadiums from his spikes for so many years. "I love the game," he said. "That's the only reason I did it."

Morgan's Catholic faith is rooted in the power of the Holy Spirit manifested through the example his parents set for him and others who helped sharpen his vision of faith during those trying years in the minor leagues. Some even were his managers when he was a young, impressionable player—men such as Del Bissonette, Bob Coleman, Ben Geraghty and Joe Schultz.

"They were good, solid men," said Morgan. "They went to Mass every Sunday, and they took their Catholic faith seriously."

Morgan played briefly in the big leaguers with Hall of Fame second baseman Red Schoendienst, one of the people Morgan admires most in baseball. "Red is a down-to-earth, regular guy," said Morgan. "He was a great player and he has always known how to relate to people."

Schoendienst recalls that Morgan was steady, both on and off the field. "Joe was quiet," said Schoendienst, who managed the Cardinals to a World Series victory over the Red Sox in 1967. "He never spouted off. He was attentive, a good listener and he got everything out of his ability. Joe is a quality person. When I looked around at Mass, Joe was always one of the guys I saw in church."

Courtesy of Joe Morgan

Joe and wife, Dot, horsing around during his minor league days.

While raising a family, the Morgans enrolled all four of their children in Blessed Sacrament Elementary School. When both were young, Dot sang in the choir during the years that Joe was an altar boy. As for their romance, it was love at first sight; Morgan was smitten immediately by Dot's charms.

"Joe told me he made up his mind right away that I was the girl he was going to marry," reported Dot. "He knew exactly where my family sat in church and how many hats and coats I had. He even told me later which ones he liked and which ones he didn't."

As a boy, Morgan shoveled snow and mowed lawns to pick up a few dollars. "I'll never forget the time my friends and I found a field filled with bottles," said Morgan, laughing as he spoke. "Anytime we wanted ice cream, we would go and collect bottles from that field and cash them in at the grocery store."

Cashing in bottles was easier on the back than shoveling snow or mowing lawns. After all, aspiring young ball players had to take care of their bodies.

Walpole, a Boston suburb where the Morgans have lived their entire lives, has given the family stability, a secure nest to live and raise a family. "Despite all the traveling during the many years in baseball, Joe and I always knew we would be going home to Walpole," said Dot.

Joe's unpretentious manner endears him to people in and out of baseball. "Joe never feels that he is above anyone, no matter who they are—the president of the United States or the guys standing on the street corner—Joe treats everyone the same," according to Dot.

In many ways, Morgan will always be a wide-eyed boy forever playing ball on the fields of dreams of his youth. Morgan once borrowed a page from the Babe Ruth legend and took part in a hot dog eating contest during spring training. "I stopped counting after Joe had consumed fourteen hot dogs," said Dot, the unofficial scorekeeper.

There's more to Morgan than baseball. He enjoys tending his vegetable garden, making jams and jellies and eating cookies. "We call him the 'Cookie Monster,' " said Dot. "Not a single cookie is safe with him around."

One time, after the Morgans spent an afternoon picking wild berries, Joe decided to make jelly in the middle of the night—at 2 A.M. to be precise. Dot recalled the incident. "I had the covers pulled over my head when Joe came into the bedroom and wanted to know where a particular pan was in the kitchen cabinet," she said.

Morgan could be any Joe living next door anywhere in America—a regular guy who rakes leaves, goes to the dump every Saturday and stops into the local donut shop after buying the morning newspaper.

He should be proud of his legacy—a devoted father, husband and a career baseball man who dedicated his life to the game. Father Maurice O'Connor, former pastor at Blessed Sacrament, admires Morgan's uncompromising loyalty to all that he loves.

"Joe Morgan is faithful to his family, his friends, his sport, his community, his Church and his God," said Father O'Connor.

Stan Musial

Stan 'The Man'

On July 3, 1988, there was an extra "Cardinal" in Rome for the canonization of a saint. On that date, Stan Musial, legendary Hall of Fame baseball player for the St. Louis Cardinals, and his wife, Lillian, attended the canonization Mass for Saint Rose Phillippine Duchesne. Mother Duchesne introduced Catholic School education west of the Mississippi River. She began her career in 1818 as a pioneer educating Catholic youth when she established a mission school for American Indians at St. Charles, Missouri.

The Musials had a particular interest in the canonization because Mother Duchesne lived and worked in the St. Louis area and because the couple's three daughters—Gerry, Janet and Jean—were educated at Villa Duchesne, a St. Louis Catholic girls' school.

It is fair to say that Stan Musial is one of the most widely loved baseball players in the history of the game. No less a personage than the late author James Michener who once said that Musial "is the most genial man in America." To those who know him, it is not surprising that one of the game's great hitters would be associated with good, even the quintessential good that embodies the canonization of a saint.

"Everyone loves Stan Musial," said Bowie Kuhn, the former Baseball Commissioner, who also is a devout Catholic. "He is so full of life and decency, and he possesses such a sweet personality."

Harry Caray, the late gruff-speaking but warm-hearted broadcaster, mentioned Musial's interior qualities, not just his superb baseball abilities. "He carried himself with unmistakable dignity, both on and off the field," said Caray. "It is his character, the soul of the man that stands out."

Musial, an outfielder and first baseman, was a feared hitter, perhaps, the greatest player in the history of the Cardinals. It is, however, the person between the number "6" on his back and the scripted "Cardinals" pressed against his chest that makes him so special.

In front of Busch Memorial Stadium, there is a statue of Musial hitting in his trademark crouched, corkscrew batting stance. The tribute to the left-handed slugger reads: "Here stands baseball's perfect warrior and perfect knight."

As a player, he was a legend. During twenty-two seasons in the big leagues, all with the Cardinals, Musial's career batting average was a lusty .331. He collected 3,630 hits, had 475 home runs and drove in 1,951 runs. He won seven batting titles and three Most Valuable Player awards. In 1969, he was voted into the Baseball Hall of Fame.

Stan was Mary and Lukasz Musial's oldest son. His mother was of Czechoslovakian descent, and his father was a Polish-American. There were

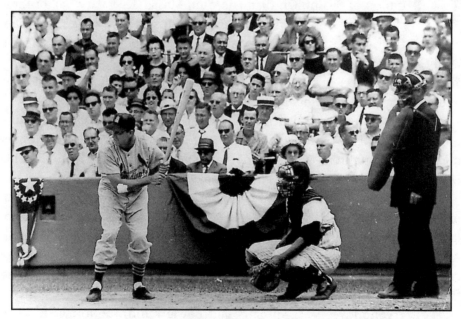

National Baseball Hall of Fame, Cooperstown, NY and Fred Roe

Musial showcasing his trademark "corkscrew" batting stance.

four Musial girls before Stan and his younger brother, Eddie, came along. Musial grew up in Denora, Pennsylvania, twenty-eight miles south of Pittsburgh. His father named him Stanislaus, which was later changed to Stanley, and nicknamed him "Stashu." His first toy was a baseball his mother made out of twine, and he quickly became a Pirates fan.

Lukasz Musial worked at a wire mill, and both parents labored to provide for their family during the Depression. "We were poor," recalled Musial, "but I never knew it. There was always something to eat—cabbage soup, cabbage salad, steamed cabbage, boiled cabbage and every other kind of cabbage. I can't even look at cabbage today."

The Musial boys experienced a loving relationship with their father. As soon as Stan and Eddie heard the 5 P.M. whistle at the wire mill, they raced down the dirt road to greet their dad. "We jumped up on Pop and hugged him and kissed him," said Musial, recalling his affection for his father.

As a baseball player, Musial's sweet, left-hand hitting swing propelled him into the Hall of Fame. However, as a southpaw youngster, he was an outcast in school who felt the sting of a ruler on his knuckles—a tactic teachers used to force natural left-handers to write with their right hands. He also remembered priests at St. Mary's in Denora pulling his hair and pinning his ears back for not knowing the correct answer in catechism classes.

By the time he was well into his teens, Musial had developed into a superb all-around athlete. Sadly, his abilities and career plans caused a rift between him and his father. More than anything, his father wanted him to attend college. In fact, he was offered a basketball scholarship to attend the University of Pittsburgh, but Stan had other ideas. He loved baseball and he wanted to become a big league ball player.

Confused and not wanting to upset his father, he sought the advice of Helen Kloz, a librarian at Denora High School. After listening to his story, the wise woman told him: "Stan, I have never seen anyone want anything more than you want to play professional baseball, so my advice is to go with what is in your heart."

She must have been a Cardinals' fan.

As difficult as it was to disappoint his father and go against his wishes, Musial courageously decided to follow his own star. "It was very hard," recalled Musial. "My father did not speak to me for a few years."

It took a long time for the wounds to heal. The acrimony between father and son persisted until Musial, then a big leaguer with the Cardinals, gave his "wide-eyed Pop" a personal tour of the Cardinal's locker room at the old Sportsman's Park in St. Louis.

In September 1941, before his 21st birthday, Musial made the jump to the big leagues and quickly became a starter in the Cardinals' outfield, one of the best in the team's history—Musial in left, Terry Moore in center and Enos "Country" Slaughter in right.

As a young ballplayer, Musial worried about having to spend so much time on the road away from his wife and baby son, Dick, who was born during the years of Musial's whirlwind rise through the minor leagues. Enter his father-in law, Sam Labash, who was a pretty good ball player in his own right. He quieted Musial's fears by telling him: "I'll watch out for your wife and baby. You play baseball and concentrate on becoming the best player you can!"

And what a player he became, a living nightmare for National League pitchers. He once hit five home runs in a doubleheader against the Giants. He had a total of six home runs in All-Star games. He reached the coveted 3,000 hit plateau with a game-winning, pinch-hit double against the Cubs at Wrigley Field.

He was cheered by crooks and cops, imitated by youth, adopted by fans in every National League park and revered by everyone from board chairmen to bus boys. Long before the Dallas Cowboys became "America's team," Stan Musial was America's favorite athlete.

The rabid Brooklyn fans actually gave him his nickname, with assistance from St. Louis sports editor Bob Broeg, who wrote the book, *Stan Musial—The Man's Own Story.*

After collecting nine hits in eleven at-bats in one series against the Dodgers at Ebbets Field, Musial went on another 11-for-15 rampage in a later series at Brooklyn. Each time he came to the plate, the crowd murmured what sounded like, "Here comes THAT man again." Broeg listened intently and what he heard was, "Here comes THE MAN again." Forever after, wherever baseball is played, Stanley Frank Musial has been known as "Stan The Man."

Musial said his greatest thrill was simply the fact that he was paid to play a game he loved. Every so often, since his retirement in 1963, he spreads his old contracts out on the kitchen table like a deck of cards and admires them.

In 1958, when the Cardinals made him the first player in the National League to earn $100,000 a year, he signed the contract without even reading it. "Hey, Stan," said the Cardinals' brass, "you better read it—it's for $100,000!" Typical of Musial, he is not the least bit resentful that he earned peanuts compared to the bloated salaries that players are paid today, many of whom could not carry Musial's spikes.

Off the field, Musial has always been accessible, pleasant and comfortable with the public. His oldest daughter, Gerry, said her father is "modest, humble, generous, fun-loving and a good guy." She also said he could be a disciplinarian. "He abhorred late sleepers, and we always had to go to early Mass on Sundays."

Musial's son, Dick, was a talented football halfback in high school who lettered in track at Notre Dame. He probably was blessed with considerable baseball talent, too. But he did not play the game. Can you blame him? No son would want to be compared to a father named Stan "The Man" Musial.

Gerry said the Sisters of the Sacred Heart and Villa Duchesne helped the Musial girls develop their own identities. "Everyone had to wear the ugliest uniforms," she said. "They didn't want us to feel that we were special just because our father was the big baseball star, Stan Musial."

Any time the Musial girls even hinted at pomposity, the nuns would ask them, "Who the heck is your father, anyway?"

"It was so totally normal," said Gerry, about life growing up in the Musial household. The Catholic faith was an unseen but ever-present and intangible part of their daily life, Gerry said. "We always knew that our Catholic faith was very important. As far back as I can remember, it was always there and it permeated the entire family."

Every November 21 the Musials celebrate two special events—Musial's birthday and the couple's wedding anniversary. "We should have married on some other day than Stan's birthday," said Mrs. Musial, who also said the couple is grateful for all their blessings, including Musial's recovery from prostate cancer.

Prior to Christmas 1988, Musial accompanied James Michener, who was awarded the Polish government's highest civilian medal for his best-selling book, *Poland*, on a fourteen-day pilgrimage to Poland and Rome. Musial, who had a field in Wroclaw, Poland renamed in his honor, conducted a baseball clinic for the Polish national team.

Watching Musial play his harmonica and perform magic tricks he learned from a traveling salesman more than fifty years ago, Michener remarked, "Stan Musial is no icon. He is a fun-loving human being who really enjoys people."

The highlight of the pilgrimage was a private Mass and dinner with Pope John Paul II. As the group assembled in the papal library waiting to be escorted into the pope's private chapel, Musial winked at those present and slyly remarked: "I'm entitled to be here because I am a 'Cardinal' too."

Jim O'Brien

An Unbeatable Team

March 3, 1991 was a beautiful Sunday. The O'Briens had just returned home from Mass, and Jim O'Brien, then head basketball coach at Boston College, was enjoying the afternoon.

His wife, Christine, was a bit miffed when he declined to go out for a walk, but O'Brien was watching a college basketball game on television, and he remained glued to the TV screen.

Christine went out for the walk without her husband, and about an hour later "I heard her come in," O'Brien said, recalling that she went straight upstairs.

His eyes began to fill with tears. "I really didn't intend to talk about this," he said.

"The next thing I heard was Christine yelling, 'Jim!' " he said.

O'Brien rushed upstairs and discovered his wife in the throes of a fatal heart attack. He quickly called 911, tried to do what he could until help arrived and then rode in the ambulance to a nearby hospital. Christine was pronounced dead shortly after she arrived at the hospital.

Christine had battled Hodgkin's disease for fifteen years. During that time, she had received radiation treatments, which left scar tissue on her heart. The scar tissue may have caused, or at least contributed to, Christine's fatal heart attack.

At the time of her death, Christine was forty-one years old. She and Jim had two teenage daughters, Erin and Amy. And Jim had a high profile, high-stress job coaching Division 1 college basketball—and his future at Boston College was the subject of debate in the media. So, O'Brien faced emotional upheaval in his career and in his home.

But O'Brien knew what his priorities were.

Courtesy of Boston College

In action at Boston College

"My first responsibility was to my daughters," he said. "I had to get a handle on what was going on at home."

As a widower, Jim had little time to grieve. Instead, he had to learn immediately to function as a single parent. Christine who, he said, was "the driving force of our family who shaped our religious attitudes," left a large role to be filled.

Before Christine's death, both he and his daughters needed a push to get out of bed and get to Sunday Mass. Christine was the one who did the pushing, according to O'Brien.

Christine had done more than make sure the family got to Sunday Mass. She had run the household, paid the bills, and to a great extent been responsible for raising the two girls.

Suddenly, all that changed. "I didn't know what bills to pay, how much life insurance we had, where to go to buy a prom dress or what to do or who to call when my daughters were going through stages in development that only women know about," he said.

When Amy, the younger of the two girls, was confirmed, O'Brien was forced to juggle his responsibilities. "I had to cut the basketball meetings short so I could rush home, prepare a pot luck supper and then make it to Amy's confirmation on time," he said.

Not many fathers are comfortable talking with their daughters about sexual issues. O'Brien is no exception. However, he did not let the issue slide. He had the courage to face it, refusing to let a difficult subject put up a wall between him and his daughters."

Fortunately, their values were well established," he said. "But I did worry about them. I told them that sex should be special, and that it is sacred only in marriage. I told them to be careful and to avoid situations where they would be tempted."

As for basic necessities like cooking, O'Brien never met a piece of meat, fish or poultry that he knew how to cook. "One day it was snowing and I was outside cooking on the grill," he admitted, sheepishly. "A neighbor saw me, came over and asked what I was doing. I told him I was cooking on the grill because I didn't know how to use a stove."

Following Christine's death, Jim and the girls decided together to seek counseling. He said that two priests at Boston College were particularly helpful and that he and his daughters leaned on each other as they attempted to piece the broken family chain back together.

"When times are good, we sometimes take things like our faith for granted," said O'Brien. "I know I did. Who do you turn to when you lose your wife and the girls lose their mother? I had a lot of questions. I needed someone to answer them. I was searching, and I guess I was looking for a more meaningful relationship with Christ."

For a husband grieving over the loss of his wife and children mourning the death of their mother, comfort sometimes is found in the unusual places. For the O'Briens, Christine's spirit manifested itself in, of all places, a family bathroom.

"I don't know how to tell you this," said O'Brien, "but for five months after Christine's death, a light bulb in one of the bathrooms was on the verge of blowing. It flickered on and off. We didn't change it. It was her [Christine]. She was there. It was her way of telling us that she was with God and that she was OK."

O'Brien is comforted by the memories that twenty years of being married to the woman he loved can provide. Of all the memories, there is one that stands out. "Christine and I kissed each other and told each other how much we loved one another every day," said O'Brien. "My girls and I do the same thing. It is very important. People need to say it, and people need to hear it, too. Every single day."

Courtesy of Boston College

An intense moment

The lesson of the importance of expressing feelings to loved ones is one that O'Brien learned the hard way. "I have lost my father, my mother and my wife," said O'Brien. "If I have one regret, it is that I don't remember telling my father and mother how much I loved them."

He tries to carry the same message to his college basketball players, telling them how best to honor their own fathers and mothers. "I ask my players," said O'Brien, "when was the last time you talked to your mother, talked to your father? If they just shrug their shoulders, I tell them to get on the telephone, call them and tell them how much they love them."

Much of O'Brien's team orientation comes from his strong family background. He is the second oldest of James and Katherine Briordy O'Brien's seven children, and he grew up in a part of Brooklyn called the Gowanus Projects.

"My father was an accountant,

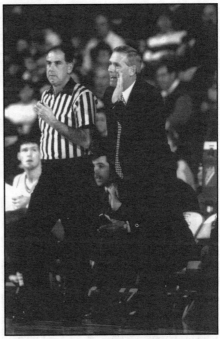

Courtesy of Boston College

Voicing words of encouragement

and he worked hard," said O'Brien. "We didn't have any extras, but we didn't want for anything, either."

At one time, when Jim's grandfather lived with the family, there were ten people living in the O'Brien home. "You know, it is funny when I think about it," recalled O'Brien, of his days growing up in Brooklyn. "All those people and we had just one bathroom. We never had a problem. With me and my girls, we had two and one-half bathrooms, and it seemed that we were always in each other's way."

As a basketball player, O'Brien, a sharp-shooting and clever ball-han-

Courtesy of Boston College

On the Eagles' sideline

dling guard, was a star in both high school and college. At Boston College, he played under Holy Cross and Boston Celtics' great Bob Cousy. He capped a superb college basketball career by being voted into the Boston College athletic Hall of Fame. As a schoolboy, O'Brien starred at St. Francis Prep, where he also is a member of the school's sports Hall of Fame.

After briefly playing professional basketball in the old ABA, Jim's first head coaching job at the college level was at St. Bonaventure. In three seasons, he guided the Bonnies to 67-51 record.

He spent eleven seasons as the head coach at Boston College, winding up with a 168-166 record. It was an up and down tenure, to say the least. However, in 1993-94, he guided the Eagles to the NCAA Regional Tournament championship game, upsetting Indiana and Kentucky in the process, and in 1996-97, his B.C. team defeated Georgetown and Villanova en route to winning the Big East Tournament Championship.

> During his final year at Boston College, O'Brien locked horns with the B.C. admissions department, which rejected student-athletes whom O'Brien had recruited. That battle weighed heavily into his decision to leave Boston College and take the position of head basketball coach at Ohio State.

During his final year at Boston College, O'Brien locked horns with the B.C. admissions department, which rejected student-athletes whom O'Brien had recruited. That battle weighed heavily into his decision to leave Boston College and take the position of head basketball coach at Ohio State.

After taking over as the head basketball coach of the Ohio State Buckeyes, O'Brien tackled a rebuilding task. In 1997-98, his first season at Ohio State, the Buckeyes finished 8-22 overall and 1-15 in the murderous Big Ten. During 1998-99, Ohio State produced one of the top college basketball stories of the year. O'Brien led the Buckeyes to a 22-7 regular season record and a second place finish in the Big Ten. The team was ranked eleventh in the country and easily qualified for the NCAA tournament.

In the NCAA Division 1 Men's Basketball Tourney, also known as March Madness, Ohio State (27-8) reeled off four straight wins, captured the South Regional Championship with a 77-74 victory over St. John's and advanced to the Final Four for the first time since 1968. As a reward, O'Brien was named Coach of the Year in the Big Ten, and he finished second in the national Coach of the Year balloting. three years earlier, while coaching at Boston College he was named Big East Co-Coach of the Year.

Jim O'Brien was the head coach at Ohio State for seven seasons, compiling a 133-88 record. He was fired following the 2003-04 season for an alleged recruiting violation.

O'Brien knows all about picking up the pieces of his life and starting fresh. When his oldest daughter, Erin, left home in the fall of 1992 to attend Stonehill College on a basketball scholarship, a fragile family unit experienced strain once again. "We shed more tears," he said, "because ever since Christine died, it had been just the three of us."

Basketball has been an important part of the lives of O'Brien and his two daughters, Erin and Amy, but it is faith and the closeness of the family unit that sustained them during the darkest of days.

Jackie Robinson

Moses in Flatbush

By definition, the word holy means to-be-set-apart. A holy person stands out because the presence of God shines through. Baseball Hall of Fame member Jackie Robinson, a physically handsome man who broke the chains of segregation in baseball, was such a man, a genuinely holy person.

He suffered fiercely, and he loved divinely. His spiritual depth—which gave him the courage and endurance to do good and conquer evil—was gloriously visible through his beaming black face. Not only was he a legendary athlete, but he was also a truly heroic human being and one of the greatest men of the twentieth or any other century.

Jackie Robinson is my all-time favorite athlete—no one else comes even close.

In 1946, when he signed with the Brooklyn Dodgers, Robinson became the first African-American to sign a contract with a major league baseball team. That season, the Dodgers assigned him to their top farm team, the Montreal Royals. During his only season playing for the Royals, Robinson carried the hopes and dreams of an entire race on his shoulders. Despite the pressure, Robinson played like a man on fire, burning with as much raw passion as any athlete who has ever competed in any sport. Jackie led the

Montreal ball club to the International League pennant and playoff championship, the World Series of minor league baseball. In the process, he was voted the league's most valuable player.

After the last out of the final championship game, which clinched the title, the overflowing Montreal crowd swarmed onto the field. Frightened, Robinson fled out of the ball park and into the street. He had won a championship for the city, and the predominantly white baseball fans idolized him. Jackie Robinson was the hero of both the English- and French-speaking Montreal fans.

Shouts of "Jackie! Jackie! Jackie!" rang in his ears. People grabbed and pulled him, but he managed to escape. Finally, safe inside his apartment, the realization of what had happened struck him, and he was overcome with emotion. A mostly white crowd had raced after him, a black man, not to lynch him but to lionize him. As the awareness grew of the significance of this event, he wept. Prayer and perseverance squeezed a moment of joy out of tremendous trials and daily pressures. Robinson triumphed—prayer had given him the strength he needed.

But baseball was an ordeal. At Montreal and during his rookie season with the Brooklyn Dodgers in 1947, Robinson would periodically tell his wife, Rachel: "I've had enough. I can't go on. I'm going to quit. I can't take anymore."

Then he and Rachel would drop to their knees, and from the very depths of their beings, they would ask God for strength. He never quit. He always played another day.

And so Jackie Robinson continued to be a bright light, not only for his people, but also for the entire country.

Jackie and Rachel were soul mates, an unbeatable team united in a Christian marriage, and together they faced the hatred and prejudice that barred blacks from being first-class citizens—not only in baseball, but also everywhere in America where there was segregation, where blacks were denied the right to vote, or discriminated against in employment, housing, and educational opportunities. To the white world, he was just an exceptionally gifted natural athlete and ball player. However, to his own people, he was oh-so-much more, a modern day Moses who clearly was God's anointed one.

Jack Roosevelt Robinson was twenty-eight years old by the time he made it to the big leagues. He was a sensational all-around athlete at UCLA—

a record-setting broad jumper, a basketball star, a break-away football half-back and an excellent baseball player, although he probably was more talented in the other sports.

As a Dodger, Robinson wore number 42. That was a number usually assigned to pitchers and not one for an infielder. He had a pigeon-toe walk, and he spoke in a high-pitched, shrill voice. He had strong, sloping shoulders, and when he stood at the plate in a medium-wide, semi-open stance, he held the bat high, almost defiantly over his right shoulder.

He was a terror on the base paths. If he got to first base, he would take an aggressive lead off the bag, sometimes shifting his weight from side to side, dancing on the balls of his feet, and sometimes he would stand motionless in the sunlight with his hands on his hips, as if mocking the pitcher and daring him to throw the ball. His explosive dashes on the base paths, especially his thundering thefts of home plate, produced some of the most exhilarating moments in baseball history. In the first game of the 1955 World Series, won by the Yankees, 6-5, Robinson stole home in the eighth inning, slicing the New York lead to a single run.

> He was a terror on the base paths. If he got to first base, he would take an aggressive lead off the bag, sometimes shifting his weight from side to side, dancing on the balls of his feet, and sometimes he would stand motionless in the sunlight with his hands on his hips, as if mocking the pitcher and daring him to throw the ball. His explosive dashes on the base paths, especially his thundering thefts of home plate, produced some of the most exhilarating moments in baseball history.

With Hall of Famer Whitey Ford on the mound, Robinson danced off third base, threatening to steal home. Suddenly, in a flash, the dancing turned into a mad dash toward the plate, startling the Yankees. I can still see him rumbling like a runaway buffalo down the line. The ball arrived to catcher Yogi Berra as Robinson stretched out in a long, graceful slide, sending dirt flying.

It was a bang-bang play. Berra applied the tag. The umpire called Robinson safe. Berra wheeled and went into a tantrum, jawing with the umpire, certain that Robinson was out.

Berra was right, too. Clearly, the replays, which I have seen hundreds of times, showed that Berra had actually nailed Robinson, tagging him before his foot touched the plate. It was one of those dramatic plays in baseball history that people will talk about as long as there are bats and balls.

The Dodgers, as many remember, rallied from two games down in 1955 to win their only World Series Championship in Brooklyn. In the seventh and deciding game, Johnny Podres, aided by Sandy Amoros' nifty grab of Berra's drive into the left field corner in the sixth inning, shut out the Dodgers, 2-0. Gil Hodges drove in both runs and Podres, who won two games in the Series, was the MVP.

The parade and celebration that followed turned Brooklyn upside down. Forty-four years later, if you close your eyes and listen intently, you can still hear the commotion.

Robinson was the National League Rookie of the Year in 1947 and the Most Valuable Player in 1949 when he led the league in batting with a .342 average, had 203 hits, 16 home runs, 124 runs batted in and a league-leading 37 stolen bases. During his career, he was an All-Star six times. During his ten seasons with the Dodgers, he had a .311 career batting average. And remember, he did not get to the Majors until he was twenty-eight. If he had been white, he would have started in the Majors eight or nine years earlier. His record would have been even more phenomenal.

But at any age, Jackie Robinson was a winner. He was one of the greatest clutch performers in sports history. He helped lead the Dodgers to seven pennants and one World Series Championship. As great an athlete as he was, he was an even bigger man. It is his indomitable spirit that will endure long after games are no longer played. That's why Jackie Robinson is unforgettable, even today more than half a century since he broke in with the Dodgers.

Branch Rickey, the president of the Dodgers, was the man who had the courage to challenge prejudice in baseball. But he needed the right player to break the color line. So the maverick baseball executive searched for someone with character, faith and high morals as well as a superbly gifted athlete. He found all of that and more in Jackie Robinson.

Near the end of the first face-to-face meeting between the two men, Rickey handed Robinson a book on the life of Christ and told him to read it. Jackie did just that, and he struggled to imitate Jesus and to apply the lessons of Jesus' life to his own. It took both time and grace for him to accept the truth—that to succeed he would have to imitate Christ in turning the other cheek and accepting insults and hatred of others without retaliating.

At one point in their conversation, Robinson screamed at Rickey: "Do you want a ball player who is afraid to fight back?"

Looking intently at Robinson, from beneath his scraggly eyebrows, Rickey sternly answered: "I chose you because I think you are man enough not to fight back!"

From our vantage point, it is inconceivable that blacks would never have broken the racial barriers which barred them from professional sports. Without Robinson, someday surely, they would have overcome. But with Jackie Robinson, they overcame before schools were desegregated, while Jim Crow still ruled in the South, when there were "whites only" water fountains, and the law consigned blacks to the back of the bus. He persevered because of his strength of character, his humility in the face of those who would humiliate him, his bravery when his physical well-being and even his life were threatened, his courage and commitment to excellence when he had the only black face in Major League Baseball. Baseball's great experiment, which is how easing blacks into professional baseball was viewed more than fifty years ago, would have failed had Robinson not willingly (fiat—let it be done) followed the will of God and embraced horrific suffering so that others could experience new life.

Ironically, a southern-born teammate, the late Hall of Famer Pee Wee Reese, was one of the first to support Robinson during his rookie season, the summer of 1947 when Jackie was the loneliest fish in the biggest fish bowl in America.

Reese, who was the Dodger captain, gave Jackie the kind of solidarity he needed and craved most. "Hey, Pee Wee," shouted opponents, "What are the good folks back home going to say when they find out you are playing beside a 'nigger'?"

Pee Wee was nicknamed "the Kentucky Colonel" and he wore number 1. He silenced Robinson's abusers by walking over to Jackie and putting his arm around his teammate's shoulders. In terms of unity and singleness of purpose, it might have been the most meaningful embrace in the history of professional baseball.

Clay Hooper, a Mississippian who was Robinson's manager at Montreal, experienced a total change of heart toward African-Americans because of all that Robinson's life taught him. Before he met Jackie, his ignorance was so deeply ingrained that he questioned whether or not blacks were even human beings. However, after getting to know Jackie, day after day during a long and at times seemingly endless baseball season, Hooper underwent a personal conversion and he became one of Robinson's ardent champions.

The axiom: "it takes a good woman to produce a strong man" is doubly true in Robinson's case. Two wonderful women gave him indispensable support in his life. Rachel, his wife, supported him through his agonizing baseball ordeal. But it was his mother, Mallie McGriff Robinson, who gave him his first lessons in courage. When she was left to raise five children by herself, she boldly moved the family from Georgia to California where there was more opportunity. She taught all of her children the primary importance of prayer, and she pieced together a better life for her family by working her fingers to the bone and filling in whatever cracks there were in their lives with love.

Jackie Robinson possessed many saintly qualities, including his zeal, his indomitable spirit, his courage, and his pursuit of good and his abhorrence of evil. At the same time, he was no plastic saint. Jack was hugely human. He fought to control a frightful temper; he was as stubborn as a mule; and he found it difficult to forgive. He also battled obesity for much of his life.

Rachel, a feminine powerhouse who later taught nursing at Yale, shared all of Jackie's triumphs and his tragedies, including the death of their son, Jackie, Jr., in an automobile accident after he had battled back from drug addiction. Rachel Robinson is a convert to Catholicism. She was the keynote speaker at the 1991 Boston College commencement, and she heads the Jackie Robinson Foundation which provides scholarships to needy students.

Jackie Robinson possessed many saintly qualities, including his zeal, his indomitable spirit, his courage, and his pursuit of good and his abhorrence of evil. At the same time, he was no plastic saint. Jack was hugely human. He fought to control a frightful temper; he was as stubborn as a mule; and he found it difficult to forgive. He also battled obesity for much of his life.

Jackie was voted into the baseball Hall of Fame in 1962. After he retired from baseball, he continued to be a crusader for the causes that were dear to him—equality and justice. His passionate appeals were listened to by presidents, senators, governors, labor leaders and civil rights advocates.

In the end, he suffered from heart disease and diabetes, and he was legally blind. By the time he died on October 24, 1972, at age fifty-three, Jackie's hair had turned snow white, perhaps because he had given all that he had to fight the good fight.

Truly to whom much is given, much is expected. Jackie Robinson received much and gave all.

"He was a battler," said former Boston Red Sox slugger and current Angels star Mo Vaughn. "He opened doors beyond baseball. That's why I wear number 42. I wear it to pay tribute to Jackie Robinson."

Incidentally, major league baseball dedicated the 1997 season to the memory of Jackie Robinson, fifty years after he became the first African-American to play major league baseball. Following that season, his number 42 was officially retired.

On earth and in heaven!

Red Schoendienst

The Redhead,
The Trolley,
and St. Louis

The unofficial first sports player agent was a warm-hearted Irish woman named Mary Eileen Theresa. Her maiden name was O'Reilly. Her married name was Schoendienst.

And for more than a half-century, until her death in 1998, she was the wife of Hall of Fame second baseman Albert Fred "Red" Schoendienst. During his illustrious career, Red, old number "2" did the playing, while Mary handled the purse strings and kept the home fires burning. "Red would have played for nothing if my father and I hadn't stepped in and negotiated his contract for him," said Mary.

The Schoendiensts' romance had a "dreamy" beginning. Mary explained: "I had a dream that I would meet a ballplayer with red hair," she said. "Actually, in the dream, he was my tutor. I kept noticing that he had red hair underneath his baseball cap."

Shortly thereafter, Mary and a German-American friend, who also was named Mary, hopped on a streetcar and headed for old Sportsman's Park in St. Louis to watch a Cardinals baseball game.

During the game, Mary saw that the Cardinals' second baseman, Schoendienst, was a redhead. After the game, the girls hung around near the entrance to the Cardinals' clubhouse, and a few of the players signed autographs for the fans. Red, however, was not among them. As the girls climbed aboard the streetcar and headed home, Mary asked her German-American friend how Schoendienst, a German-Dutch-American, pronounced his name.

Once, twice, three times Mary asked her friend the same question. After all, Schoendienst, can be as tricky to pronounce as it is to spell. After the third inquiry, her friend was startled to see who was standing behind them on the trolley. "Turn around," she blurted. "Red Schoendienst is standing right behind you!"

Mary and Red's romance blossomed quickly, and St. Margaret's Church in St. Louis became a place where they met. One day after Mass, Red asked Mary for her telephone number and she obliged. "That's when I gave him my autograph," said Mary, laughing as she remembered the beginning of their courtship that led to marriage and a lifetime commitment.

Mary's father was a postal clerk named James Patrick O'Reilly. Two of his greatest loves were Notre Dame football and the Redbirds—the St. Louis Cardinals. "I first heard about Red—a new kid playing second base for the Cardinals—from my father," said Mary.

The Schoendiensts were married at St. Margaret's on October 13, 1947. Many of Red's teammates attended the wedding. Mary's father, Mr. O'Reilly, sold the family car and cashed in saving bonds to pay for the reception. "Red paid my father back," said Mary, who doubled as the family accountant.

Red Schoendienst grew up in Germantown, Illinois, a small community of about 600 people fifty miles from St. Louis. His parents, Joseph and Mary, had seven children; six boys and one girl. Red was in the middle of the brood. He grew up during the Depression. Times were tough and his father, whom Schoendienst called "a real utility man," found work wherever he could. He was a carpenter as well as a coal miner, and he regularly left for work at four in the morning and did not return until well after dark.

Germantown, like so many small towns throughout the Midwest, was a tightly knit community. "Everyone worked," remembered Schoendienst. "You helped farmers with their wheat and oats. People were neighborly and no one locked their doors at night."

In his youth, Red recalls trudging to nearby St. Bonafice Church to attend daily Mass. He also was enrolled at the parish elementary school. The family prayed the rosary, especially during Lent, and just about everybody was interested in baseball. "A cattle truck was our team bus," he said. "We cleaned out the back every Sunday. Even when I was just a kid, I remember climbing onto the back of that truck and traveling to baseball games all over the county."

During his first season in professional baseball, Red dislocated a shoulder crashing into a fence, and for the rest of his career the injury caused him pain, especially when he was the middle or pivot-man attempting to turn or complete a double play. "I always had a sore arm after that," he said.

Throughout his Hall of Fame career, Schoendienst started each season like a house on fire. Then, as the summer heat intensified, the switch-hitting second sacker wilted like a rose. "I started to wear down every season around July," he said.

After years of fighting mid-season listlessness, Schoendienst finally had a series of tests that revealed he had tuberculosis. He entered a hospital and

St. Louis Globe Democrat

Schoendienst taking a high throw at second base.

underwent an operation that removed part of a lung following a memorable 1957 season.

In 1956, after playing ten-plus seasons with the Cardinals, Red was traded from the Cardinals to the New York Giants. Then, fifty-seven games into the 1957 season, he was dealt to Milwaukee to shore up the Braves' infield during a pennant-winning season. As most baseball fans know, in 1957 the Braves appeared in the World Series for the first time since 1948, when the team was based in Beantown and was known as the Boston Braves. The Braves won the '57 World Series by outlasting the New York Yankees. The number one hero was right-hander Lou Burdette, who won three Worlds Series games. Schoendienst hit .278 in the '57 Series and .300 in the '58 Series, which the Yankees won 6-2 when Bob Turley pitched a complete game in the deciding game.

With the help of expert medical attention plus the power of prayer, Schoendienst completely recovered from tuberculosis. Prayers were offered for him by Catholics, young and old, all across the country. Red and Mary Schoendienst cherish the memory of the outpouring of support. "I still have boxes of cards and letters that were sent to Red when he was in the hospital," Mary said. "Catholic school children, nuns, priests, and fans everywhere were praying for Red's recovery."

For eleven seasons, Schoendienst roomed with another Hall of Fame player, Stan "The Man" Musial. Both men share similar values and interests. "We were very compatible," said Red. "Stan and I have always been like brothers."

The Schoendiensts sent all four of their children, three girls and a boy, to Catholic schools. In many Catholic families blessed with three daughters, the odds are that one of them will be named Mary in honor of the Blessed Mother. Red and his wife have not one, but three Mary's—Mary Colleen, Mary Kathleen and Mary Eileen—plus a son, Kevin Albert.

Meals have always been a special time for prayer in the Schoendiensts' home, and Mary said that all their children practice and remain loyal to their Catholic faith. "Life is not easy for young people," said Mary, after she suffered a stroke in 1990 but recovered. "All people, regardless of age, need their faith today more than ever."

At the time she said that the Schoendiensts always counted their blessings, adding, "God has been very good to us."

In retirement, Red, who continues his many years of association with the Cardinals, is an avid hunter, although Mary did not share his enthusiasm for the sport. "I get provoked by the amount of time Red spends hunting," she once said. "But it is one of his passions. He just loves the outdoors."

As a player, Schoendienst, who broke in with the Cardinals as a pencil-thin, spray-hitting infielder, played nineteen seasons in the big leagues. He posted a .289 career batting average and had 2,449 hits. Red played on two World Series Championship ball clubs, and he won the 1950 All Star game for the National League with a dramatic 14th-inning home run off Detroit Tiger's pitcher Ted Gray at the old Comisky Park in Chicago. He also managed the Redbirds to the 1967 World Series title against the Red Sox.

Over the years, Red's waistline has expanded, but not as much as today's bloated baseball salaries. "With the money these guys are making," said Schoendienst. "I would still be playing if I could get my weight down to 170 pounds."

Courtesy of the Dallas Cowboys

Roger Staubach

The Ultimate Touchdown

He captured the Heisman Trophy as a junior at the U.S. Naval Academy. A brilliant athlete, he was known for his skill, leadership and daring. He was the author of the legendary "Hail Mary" pass that claimed one of the most thrilling finishes in the history of the NFL play-offs. And fittingly, he was elected to the Pro Football Hall of Fame after a fabulous career with the Dallas Cowboys.

But Roger Staubach's goal is an imperishable one—eternal salvation — a touchdown scored not in this world, but in heaven, where the cheering goes on forever.

Born on February 5, 1942, fifty-seven year old Staubach is a husband, father, grandfather, and CEO of the Staubach Company, a Dallas based commercial real estate firm. As a committed Catholic, he delicately balances his life between the temporal and the eternal. In fact, he lives each day in the context of eternity.

The former quarterback great has grown spiritually to the point where he is humbled, flattened harder than any blind-side blitz his body absorbed during his playing days, by the unfathomable mystery of faith that challenges all believers.

"Most of us don't work as hard at our spiritual goals, at developing a relationship with Jesus Christ, as we do at other things," said Staubach. "If Christ tapped me on the shoulder today, would I change? Would my life be different?"

To deepen his own relationship with the Lord, Staubach goes directly to the source, namely Sacred Scripture. Since 1973, he has blocked out time each day for prayer and Bible study.

"Sacred Scripture poses many difficult questions," Staubach continued. "We don't have the answers to many of those questions. Faith is what fills the void. I have an engineering degree from Annapolis. I am a methodical person with a clinical mind. I am used to looking for and finding answers, except when it comes to matters of faith."

As he travels his own pilgrim journey of faith, confronted and often confounded by the verities of life, Staubach marvels at an important Biblical paradox. As much as men quest for power and wealth, in the final analysis, it is to those who are disposed as a child to whom the keys of God's kingdom are given.

"If we truly listen to God's word, child-like faith and trust in God is what it takes to reach heaven," said Staubach.

Father Joseph Ryan was a Catholic chaplain at the Naval Academy when Staubach was a plebe. He still remembers the first time he met Staubach. "He hadn't even been sworn in yet," remembered Father Ryan. "At the time, I was introduced to seven young men. The last one I met was Roger. The others shook my hand and made polite remarks. Roger immediately asked me what time I was saying Mass the next morning."

Daily Mass was scheduled at 0530, Navy time. Despite a hectic schedule, Staubach began participating at daily Mass the next morning at the non-denominational Annapolis chapel where the remains of John Paul Jones are entombed. "Roger was the first plebe to attend daily Mass," said Father Ryan, a close family friend who baptized four of the five Staubach children. "He regularly served as my altar boy. Others followed him, and after a short time, there were more than one hundred Midshipmen at daily Mass."

Staubach takes part in the Eucharist whenever possible. During his eleven year National Football League career, priests were recruited to say Sunday Mass at the hotels where the Cowboys stayed when the team was on the road. The late Most Reverend John McNamara, an Auxiliary Bishop of the Archdiocese of Boston and former chief of Navy chaplains, remembered a

Mass he celebrated in Washington, D.C. on the morning of a Cowboys-Redskins game at R.F.K. Stadium.

Staubach introduced himself and he immediately made his Mass intentions known. Surprisingly, his prayerful petitions had little to do with the outcome of a football game, even though the battle pitted the Cowboys against their bitter rivals, the Redskins. "Roger told me his desire to attend Mass had nothing to do with the outcome of the game," said Bishop McNamara. "He told me he wanted to attend Mass and to receive the Eucharist, because on days he didn't attend Mass and receive the Eucharist, he didn't feel like himself, that there was something missing and he experienced a void or emptiness in his life."

That afternoon the Cowboys lost to the Redskins. Bishop McNamara laughed while reporting that Staubach, true to his word, asked him to say another Mass the next year when the Cowboys once again were in the Nation's Capital to play the Redskins. "After they lost, I really thought he might want another priest to say the Mass the following year," said Bishop McNamara.

However, as the bishop and all who know Staubach will confirm, Roger's commitment to his Catholic faith transcends all sports, even football.

As a player, Staubach experienced many more wins than losses. In fact, he is such a fierce competitor that he hates to lose on a football field, in business or in a neighborhood pickup basketball game. At the same time, Roger is just as competitive, just as involved and focused, in the spiritual realm as he is in the material. For him, every day is game day, both an opportunity to deepen his relationship with the Lord and a challenge to choose good over evil in all his affairs.

Drew Pearson, the Cowboys' all-time leading receiver with 489 recep-

Courtesy of the United States Naval Academy

Midshipman Staubach

tions covering more than 7,000 yards and accounting for forty-eight touch-downs, played seven seasons in the NFL with Staubach. The two men remain close friends and have deep respect for each other. "Roger is a quality person," said Pearson. "He is morally and ethically sound. I learned a lot about football from Roger, but he taught me just as much about what's really important in life, including how to get along with people."

Pearson also said that Staubach leads by example and he never preaches or forces his beliefs on others. "He enhances others," explained Pearson. "Just being around him as a teammate you become a better player, and outside of football he makes you try to become a better person. It all comes from the kind of example he sets.

"It just overflows from the kind of person that he is. He is a leader. He has earned that distinction. Roger is down to earth; he is very human. He can be very witty. He has great work habits and he is real."

During Staubach's storybook football career, first at Navy, where he was the finest quarterback in the rich history of Naval Academy football, and later in the NFL, he made life miserable, more often than not, for the opposition.

Courtesy of the United States Naval Academy

En route to capturing the Heisman Trophy

During his NFL career, the Cowboys were adopted by legions and known as "America's Team." Staubach was nicknamed "Roger the Dodger" and "Captain America." The nicknames were well earned. The scrambling, go-for-broke, game-breaker completed 1,685 passes for 22,700 yards and 153 touchdowns during his NFL career.

At times, especially during "crunch time" when the game's outcome was on the line, Staubach appeared to possess super-human abilities, instincts and savvy. During his NFL career, he quarterbacked the Cowboys to four Super Bowls, including victories in Super Bowl VI and Super Bowl XII. He also engineered twenty-three fourth-quarter comeback wins, including fourteen during the final two minutes of the game or in overtime.

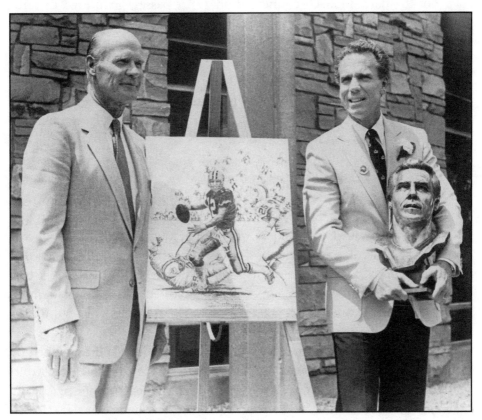

Courtesy of Father Joseph Ryan

The Inauguration of Excellence

Roger Staubach (right) with former Dallas Cowboys head coach Tom Landry at Staubach's induction into the Hall of Fame.

The crown jewel of all the comebacks that Staubach engineered took place on December 28, 1975 at the old Municipal Stadium in Minneapolis on a frigid day when the temperature never rose above twenty-seven degrees and biting winds made it seem even colder. It was the Cowboys against the Vikings with the winner advancing to the NFC title game.

With thirty-two seconds left in the game and the Cowboys trailing, 14-10, Staubach uncorked a bomb, a pass that traveled over sixty yards from the spot where he fired it. Staubach's friend and wide receiver, Pearson, made a juggling catch deep along the near sideline. He caught the ball, miraculously, inside the five yard-line, stumbled, but somehow managed to fall backwards into the end zone for the winning touchdown.

For the day, Staubach connected on 17-29 passes, good for 246 yards and one touchdown. Pearson grabbed four of those aerials, accounting for ninety-one yards, including a fifty-yarder, the game-winning play that came to be known as the "Hail Mary" pass.

The next week, the Cowboys, a wild card team, clouted the Los Angeles Rams, 37-7, to win the NFC Championship and advance to the Super Bowl. In the NFC title game, Staubach put on an air show, connecting on 16-26 passes for 220 yards and four touchdowns.

In the Super Bowl, which was played in Miami's Orange Bowl, on January 18, 1976, Dallas led 10-9 in the fourth quarter, but the Steelers rallied and won the game, 21-17. Pittsburgh wide receiver Lynn Swann was the game's number one star. Staubach completed 15-24 passes for 204 yards and two touchdowns. He also proved he was human by throwing three interceptions. Roger was voted into the Pro Football Hall of Fame in 1985, his first year of eligibility. He was the most popular quarterback of his era, a true hero—a man beyond reproach, respected and admired for his inner strength, towering faith and time-tested character as much as he was cheered for his athletic brilliance.

As for his personal life, it is rooted in commitment and nourished by grace. In September 1999, Roger and Marianne Staubach celebrated their thirty-fourth wedding anniversary. The two have known each other practically their entire lives, and their relationship dates back to when both were fourth-graders in a parochial school in Cincinnati.

Marianne knows her husband better than anyone. She characterizes him "as determined and honest, a man of perseverance and a person totally dedicated to his beliefs." She also said that his drive and seemingly limitless energy are fueled by his faith. "His impetus comes from his Catholic faith. It originates deep down inside him and it is the source of his strength."

She also revealed a human side of the man that few know. Throughout his life, Staubach has struggled with loneliness. While Marianne comes from a family of five children, Roger, who has lost both his parents, is an only child. "It was very hard for him," explained Marianne. "He was very close to his father and mother. As an only child, he doesn't have siblings to say things like, 'Remember when we used to do this or when Dad or Mom took us there?' When he talks about his youth, there is no one else to corroborate his stories. We believe him, of course, but it's not the same when you don't have brothers and sisters."

Her husband also found it difficult to express his emotions, Marianne said. But that changed in the process of raising children. He had to learn to be present for his kids while listening to them and communicating with them.

"You know how teenagers are. Sometimes they're off on another planet. Watching other members of his household go through their teenage years was a new experience for Roger. And he found it hard," Marianne said.

What lies ahead for Roger Staubach? He is a highly successful business-man. But he has never lost his strong competitive spirit. Down the road he could coach or become deeply involved in lay ministry, or he could, as has been rumored for some time, run for public office.

In answer to widespread speculation about his entry into the political arena, Staubach said: "There is nothing imminent. Everything would be determined by the opportunity and my availability. The timing would also have to be right, and if it were, politics would not be out of the question. Ultimately, it would be a decision Marianne and I would make together."

In the meantime, Roger Staubach will stay true to himself by remaining firmly rooted in the truths of the Catholic faith and keeping his eyes on the one goal line that really counts.

Part Three

In Perspective

"Touchdown Jesus"
University of Notre Dame, South Bend, Indiana

Shake Down The Thunder

Looking out from Notre Dame Stadium, you see a huge mosaic of the risen Christ with arms uplifted, which adorns the Father Theodore M. Hesburgh Library—the world's largest collegiate library building.

The mosaic is known worldwide as "Touchdown Jesus."

Perhaps some may think that irreverent. But the name combines two of the essential elements of the University of Notre Dame—Jesus and football.

It may be significant that the mosaic is not the highest point on campus. That honor goes to the 230-foot high cross on top of the bell tower of the Basilica of the Sacred Heart.

The campus has come a long way since Father Edward Sorin, C.S.C., a French priest who was a member of the Congregation of the Holy Cross, founded the University of Notre Dame in 1842. At the time, the campus consisted of three log cabins. Now, there are about eighty-eight buildings on campus and, with an operating budget of more than $400 million and an endowment approaching $2 billion. Notre Dame ranks among the nation's top twenty-five universities.

I had visited Notre Dame twice before my visit in 1998. The first time was in 1951 when I was only seven. My father, an Army captain, had been recalled to active duty during the Korean War, and my family was forced to relocate to Gary, Indiana. I visited for the second time just a few years ago.

Both visits took place during the summer, while the campus was quiet, two months before the start of the football season. That may have been part of the reason it took me fifty-four years, nine months and twenty days to witness my first Notre Dame football game in person. The date was October 3, 1998. Notre Dame versus Stanford. The Independent Fighting Irish versus the Cardinal of the Pacific-10 Conference. The sun did not shine on the Golden Dome that day. Instead, there were gray skies and gusting winds, but nothing—not even intermittent rain—could dampen that experience.

We sat thirty rows above the field in Section 2 of the north end zone at Notre Dame Stadium. We had a satisfactory, unobstructed view from where we watched Notre Dame defeat Stanford, 35-17. The win improved Coach Bob Davie's record to three wins and one loss. The 1998 season was a productive one for the Fighting Irish, posting a 9-2 record. The team faced Georgia Tech in the Gator Bowl, where the Yellow Jackets prevailed, 35-28.

Quarterback Jarious Jackson (number 7), a senior from Tupelo, Mississippi, was the number one star of the game. He rushed for one hundred yards on eighteen carries and scored three touchdowns. Jackson was the first Notre Dame quarterback to rush for one hundred yards since 1956, when Heisman Trophy winner Paul Hornung did it against North Carolina.

For months prior to the game, I had tried unsuccessfully to buy tickets. "Notre Dame home games are sold out for the next ten years," I was told. Finally, I had no alternative but to buy two tickets at grossly inflated prices through a ticket agency. The face value of each ticket was $26.50. I paid $420 for the pair. If I had waited one more week, I could have taken Notre Dame up on the offer to sell me tickets at face value. But I felt I had to get tickets well in advance. How could I possibly wait to the last minute and then head to South Bend without tickets?

Consequently, for tickets alone, it cost me $12 per point to watch the Fighting Irish score 34 points while beating Stanford by 18, in a game that was a rout, not nearly as close as the final score might indicate.

During football season, hotel rooms are just as scarce as Notre Dame football tickets. It took persistence, but I finally secured a motel room for two nights: the Econo Lodge, located about four miles from Notre Dame and surrounded by a plethora of fast food restaurants. Automobiles with license plates from New Jersey, Michigan, Wyoming, Ohio, Florida, Texas and Nebraska—just to name seven—were lined up outside the rooms at the Econo Lodge.

On a rainy, late Friday afternoon, our Notre Dame football weekend officially began. I called a cab and my wife and I headed to the 5 P.M. Mass at the Basilica of the Sacred Heart. On our last visit to Notre Dame, the Basilica was closed for renovations. My wife had never been inside, and it had been forty-seven years since I had prayed there.

We arrived minutes before the start of Mass. The Basilica was packed. Many of the people in attendance were students—friendly, good-looking kids, bundled in rain gear. Seeing so many youth at Mass was edifying; immediately, I felt grateful to be a Catholic and to share in a liturgy with Notre Dame students.

On January 17, 1992, Pope John Paul II raised Sacred Heart to the title of "Minor Basilica." The Basilica itself is overwhelming. Instead of praying, I just let myself be awed. The murals on the walls and ceilings are the work of

Courtesy of the University of Notre Dame

University of Notre Dame Stadium - Home of the Fighting Irish

Luigi Gregoni, a Vatican artist under Pope Pius IX, who came to Notre Dame in 1874 and spent the next seventeen years beautifying the Basilica.

Among the most striking paintings are *The Exaltation of the Holy Cross*, *The Coronation of the Virgin Mary as Queen of Heaven*, and *The Virgin Mary Appearing to St. Bernadette at Lourdes*. A mural on the ceiling above the sanctuary depicts four prophets; Moses, David, Jeremiah and Isaiah, and the four evangelists; Matthew, Mark, Luke, and John.

There is one more painting, and it is the most inspiring mural I have ever seen. It is entitled The Death of St. Joseph. The painting shows Christ cradling a dying St. Joseph close to his breast with the Blessed Mother sitting next to him, holding St. Joseph's hand. The scene is exquisitely tender; one cannot look at it without being moved.

The main altar, which was built in Paris, "flows in gold" in the flamboyant French Gothic style. Slender columns support the City of Jerusalem Tabernacle, which is crowned by the Lamb of God holding the cross. Its doors are decorated with plates bearing the names of the twelve tribes of Israel. Each of the twelve gates is guarded by an angel, and the wall is supported by twelve foundations, each bearing the name of one of the Apostles. To truly appreciate it, you would have to study the tabernacle at great length. It certainly conveys the richness of Church history.

Relics of St. Marcellus, a third century centurion, beheaded for not joining the Roman army, are buried beneath the altar, and the altar stone contains the relics of St. Stephen, the first Christian martyr, St. Sebastian and other early martyrs.

Following Mass, the bells from the oldest carillon in North America rang. It rained steadily as we walked behind the Basilica and down a set of stairs to the Grotto, a replica one-seventh the size of the French shrine where the Blessed Mother appeared to St. Bernadette. We knelt, prayed and we both lit a candle. As we knelt, I thought of Gerry Faust, the former Notre Dame football coach who prayed at the Grotto after every game, win or lose, home or away.

There is a statue of Dr. Tom Dooley, overlooking St. Joseph's Lake, just a few feet away from the Grotto. Dooley was a Notre Dame graduate and missionary doctor. Six weeks before he died of cancer, he wrote from Southeast Asia to Father Hesburgh, then president of Notre Dame. In the letter, which is reproduced as part of a memorial to the saintly humanitarian, Dooley writes of "his longing to see the Grotto again."

We walked across the campus to the Joyce Center for the pre-game pep rally. Admission was free. Blue and gold was the dominant color as thousands of faithful fans filed through the turnstiles. Everyone received posters which read, "WE ARE ND!" in gold and blue trim. The noise became deafening, but the highlight was the sight and sound of the Notre Dame band high-stepping through a tunnel and playing the Notre Dame Victory March as the players filed into the arena. It was an electrifying moment, chilling and thrilling.

Later, we walked to the on-campus Morris Inn, the home away from home for well-heeled Notre Dame alums, to use a telephone so I could call a cab for the return trip to the Econo Lodge. The taxicab business thrives in South Bend in large part because of the fares generated by Notre Dame.

The next morning, we got an early start to Notre Dame, traveling again by cab. We arrived at Notre Dame Stadium three hours before the 1:30 kick-off and bought matching panchos to protect us from the rain.

I wanted time to stand still so I could savor the moment. There was so much to see, to hear, to experience. I played a mind game. As the multitudes

Courtesy of the University of Notre Dame

Grotto of Our Lady of Lourdes

streamed by, I tried to envision where the people were from, who they were and what their lives were like. I often do that when I find myself in a crowd.

The highlight of the pre-game festivities was the arrival of the Notre Dame marching band about forty-five minutes before kickoff. "The band is coming!" people shouted to one another even before the band was in sight of the stadium. Before every home game, the band—led by the impressive Irish Guard—marches across the campus, chanting, "Here Come The Irish...Here Come The Irish!" on their way to the stadium. If you get caught up in the enthusiasm and pageantry of college football, and you like marching bands, it could not possibly get any better than this.

The Notre Dame-Stanford game was extra special for the band. It was Notre Dame Band Alumni Day, which meant that 900 band members—past and present—entertained the 80,012 fans who filled the expanded Notre Dame Stadium. The extra band members more than made up for the absence of the Stanford band, which was not welcome at Notre Dame because of past performances, including one during which the Stanford band "mocked visible symbols of Christianity and specifically Catholicism."

Wally and his wife, Mary, with the statue of Frank Leahy outside Notre Dame Stadium

In addition to Alumni Band Day, the 1998 Notre Dame-Stanford game brought together once again the unbeaten but once tied (9-0-1) 1953 Notre Dame team. That was Coach Frank Leahy's last and, perhaps, his best Fighting Irish team. Twenty-seven members of the 1953 team returned to Notre Dame for a 45th Anniversary reunion. Among the players welcomed back to Notre Dame were Heisman Trophy winner Johnny Lattner (number 14), quarterback Ralph Guglielmi (number 3), fullback Neil Worden (number 48), halfback Joe

Heap, All-American tackle Art Hunter, All-American end Don Penza, and tackle Frank Varrichone.

Thirteen members of that team went on to play professional football, and many believe the 1953 backfield—Guglielmi, Lattner, Heap and Worden—was the finest in the history of Notre Dame football.

While posting nine wins, Notre Dame defeated a string of top-20 teams, including: Oklahoma (number 5), Pittsburgh (number 15), Georgia Tech (number 4) and Southern California (number 20). Only a 14-14 tie against the Iowa Hawkeyes denied Notre Dame a perfect season. In the Iowa game, the Fighting Irish narrowly escaped with a tie, scoring a touchdown at the end of each half to pull even with Iowa. Notre Dame scored the tying touchdown with only six seconds remaining in the game on the second of two touchdown passes from Guglielmi to halfback Dan Shannon, the captain-elect of the 1954 Notre Dame team.

Controversy surrounded the tie. Two injury time-outs, which preserved precious seconds on the game clock, allowed Notre Dame to score both its touchdowns. Iowa screamed foul. To this day, no one can be certain if the injuries were real or faked. Perhaps, it was Oscar-caliber acting jobs that stopped the clock and gave Notre Dame two extra plays, both of which resulted in touchdowns.

In those days, Notre Dame did not participate in post-season bowl games. In 1953, Maryland was crowned the national champions, even though they were upset by the Oklahoma Sooners in the Orange Bowl. Four of Leahy's Notre Dame teams won national championships. To this day, many believe the 1953 Notre Dame team was the best in the country and worthy of the title of national champion.

Forty-five years later, Notre Dame easily defeated intersectional rival Stanford. Late in the game, it was announced that a Mass would begin at the Basilica of the Sacred Heart one-half hour after the football game ended. My wife and I hurried out of Notre Dame Stadium and followed the flow of people heading to the Basilica.

After Mass, we made one last stop at the Grotto and walked back across the campus to the Morris Inn to call a cab for the return trip to the Econo Lodge. It was raining. Darkness had settled. Notre Dame Stadium was illuminated by lights and the glow could be seen from far away.

The next morning we left for the train depot, headed to Chicago, where we changed trains en route to Milwaukee to visit my wife's sister, Helen. It was a beautiful day, sunny and mild. We met two older couples. Both were from California. They, too, had been at Notre Dame for the Stanford game. We talked about many things, including the glorious history of college football.

As we boarded the train for the short ride to Chicago, I could hear the sound of the Notre Dame band playing the Notre Dame Victory March in my mind. As a youth, I listened to that fight song on an old long-playing record until it became so scratchy I couldn't hear it anymore. As the train pulled out of the station, I felt in touch with that joy of my youth.

Note: The facts about the '53 Notre Dame team were taken from a story in the ND-Stanford game program entitled: "1953 Irish Came So Close." It was written by Craig Chval.

The Greatest Rivalry

On Saturday, December 7, 1996, my wife and I were among the 69,238 people who, along with President Clinton, came to Veterans Stadium in Philadelphia for the 97th Army-Navy football game.

There was a driving rain that afternoon, and the damp cold penetrated to the bone. We had been up all night, and our trip to Philadelphia had been arduous. We could have been mired in self-pity. We could have wished to be back in Massachusetts in our cozy apartment.

But we were thrilled to be at what I consider the greatest, grandest rivalry in all of sports. Indeed, I will carry this hyperbole a step further. I believe the Army-Navy Classic is football's finest hour. It is the most treasured rivalry in the history of the world. To historians, the ancient rivalries between Athens and Sparta or Rome and Carthage might overshadow the Army-Navy series, but not to me.

December 7, 1996 marked the fifty-fifth anniversary of the day that the Japanese had bombed Pearl Harbor in a sneak attack that brought the United States into World War II. Before the kickoff, stirring ceremonies marked the occasion. Navy fighter planes roared over the stadium in tribute, and prayers were offered for the thousands of servicemen who were killed at Pearl Harbor.

Our journey to Philadelphia to attend our second Army-Navy game in as many years (Army won by the tip of a bayonet, 14-13, in 1995.) began about 7:30 P.M. on Friday, December 6th, at South Station in Boston across the street from the Federal Reserve Building where my wife works.

We boarded train number 76 shortly before 10 P.M. Seven-and-one-half hours later, we arrived at the 30th Street train station in the City of Brotherly Love. Most of the city were still tucked in their beds. And we had some time on our hands.

The gates at Veterans Stadium did not open until nine o'clock that morning. (The kickoff was scheduled minutes after noon). What do you do at a municipal train station in a large American city, at five thirty in the morning, with time on your hands and nothing to do? We sat on hard benches, read, dozed and freshened up in the bathrooms.

At 7:45 A.M. sharp, we headed for Veterans Stadium—two subway changes and about ten stops away at the end of Patison Avenue. There were Cadets and Midshipmen in the subway station. The Cadets wore traditional dress gray, complete with capes, and the Midshipmen looked snappy in crisp, dress blue and white.

Courtesy of the United States Military Academy

One of the greatest sights in all of sports: the traditional Army-Navy "march on."

"Have you ever seen college-age kids look so good, so clean-cut, so sharp?" I exclaimed to my wife.

"No, I haven't, dear," she said, half agreeing with me, and half humoring me.

Because of the extra security needed due to the President's attendance, the gates did not open until 9:30 A.M. The only "boos" heard all day were for the supervisors of the gate attendants. At last, we climbed the long ramps leading to the upper deck, looking down at a corner of the end zone. Just as we settled into our seats, a man standing fifteen rows below where we sat shouted, "How's the view up there?"

"Fine," I answered. "Last year was my first Army-Navy game."

"Then you know you are in for a treat," he said, speaking as a true veteran of many Army-Navy Classics.

At exactly 09:43, there was a drum roll signaling the "march-on"—the reason we were there more than two hours before the opening kickoff.

Courtesy of the United States Military Academy

Here comes Army!
The Black Knights of the Hudson ready to battle the Midshipmen of Navy.

The West Pointers were the first to march onto the field since they were the visiting Academy. The Long Grey Line looked like legions of knights from a glorious past age. "Here they come," I shouted in my excitement.

As the first company of the Corps of Cadets marched into Veterans Stadium, the U.S. Army band played "When the Caissons Go Rolling Along." A tingle shot down my spine and I jumped to my feet, clapping as hard as I could. The Cadets formed thirty-six blocks of companies that stretched from one end zone to the other. After the squares were formed in perfect position, a deafening cheer rocked the stadium: "Gooooo Army. Beeeaaat Navy!"

Next came the Midshipmen, the home team for the 97th Army-Navy game. The Brigade marched into Veteran's Stadium as the U. S. Navy band played "Anchors Aweigh." The Middies, wearing white caps and blue over-coats, put on a stirring show. It was like seeing the foamy cap of one giant wave. They too voiced a resounding cheer. "Gooooo Navy. Beeeaaat Army!"

Prior to kickoff, Navy Seals and Army Special Forces troops parachuted out of the sky. The Cadets and Midshipmen formed tunnels through which their respective teams ran onto the field, lifted off their feet by the backslap-ping of the Corps and the Brigade. Minutes earlier, the rival captains traveled the same gauntlet, holding hands, just before the official coin toss.

This day belonged to the Cadets as they outlasted the Midshipmen, 28-24.

Army was down 21-3 early in the second quarter. But, led by the run-ning and passing of senior Texan and quarterback Ronnie McAda, the Cadets rallied. McAda ran for 134 yards and passed for 166 more. Army defeated Navy for a record-tying fifth straight year. The victory wrapped up a 10-1 reg-ular season and gave Army the most single season wins in its history. Coach Bob Sutton's team earned a spot in the Independence Bowl against Auburn. Despite a gallant second half charge by the Black Knights of Army, the Auburn Tigers won by a score of 32-29.

The 1995 and 1996 Army-Navy games were beauties. As Army drove ninety-nine yards late in the fourth quarter in 1995—eventually cashing in the winning touchdown—I remember seeing strangers holding hands, hop-ing that a gesture of solidarity would add extra muscle to Army's late-game charge. I recall a couple with ties to both Army and Navy saying, "We don't know who to cheer for. We love both Academies."

In 1997, Navy clobbered Army, 39-7. Then in 1998, Army rebounded, 34-30, winning the 99th game of the preeminent college football rivalry. Heading into the centennial game, Army holds a slim 48-44-7 lead in the series.

To me, the games are a celebration of all that is pure and unspoiled about athletics. In the stands, freshly scrubbed and closely clipped youths with shining faces—America's sons and daughters—cheer on their respective schools. At the end of both games, both won by Army, the Corps of Cadets and Brigade of Midshipmen stormed the field and swallowed up the players. Then suddenly, all the clamor stopped and the rival players, pairs of whom were seen embracing, dropped to their knees in silent prayer.

Then, just as suddenly, all rose and faced the Navy side of the field and sang, "Navy Blue and Gold," the Annapolis alma mater. Next, all did an about face, turned toward the Army side of the field and sang the West Point alma mater, which is simply titled "Alma Mater."

Winter darkness had fallen and the artificial lights of Veterans Stadium cast the field in a golden glow. For the second straight year, my eyes became wonderfully misty, and I did not mind not being able to see clearly. Each game ended with a chilling, thrilling climax, both were unforgettable.

I am an Army veteran, but only a private first class. Yet both games were spiritual experiences that made me feel good, clean and filled to-the-brim.

The Army-Navy game will always represent for me the best that sports bring out: virtue, honor, love of God, love of country, fraternity, common causes, fighting the good fight, persevering, competing hard but playing clean, cherishing teammates, respecting the opponent, and keeping your eyes fixed on the "goal line."

As a boy, I had dreamed of one day being captain of the Army football team. I followed Army teams closely, memorized the words to "On Brave Old Army Team" and I knew all about Glenn Davis, Doc Blanchard, Coach Earl "Red" Blaik, Pete Dawkins, Bob Carpenter, "The Lonesome End," Pete Vann, speedy Bob Anderson and Don Holleder, who was killed in Vietnam. However, the reality of my struggles with basic math, like Algebra II, put an end to such thoughts.

After each game, I felt a rush of warmth and I longed to share the experience with my late dad, Walter Sr.—the coach, the Hall of Fame athlete and the Army infantry captain who was wounded twice while fighting in the Battle of the Bulge.

One memory rekindled another. I thought of the times my father sang college football fight songs to me in the car as we drove to high school football games so he could scout future opponents. There is the lingering memory of a weekday afternoon, shortly before my father died, when the two of us sat in a half-empty darkened theatre. We lost ourselves in "Rudy," the heart-warming movie about the kid from a steel town in the Midwest who battled his way onto the Notre Dame football team.

Perhaps going to that movie together was a way for us to communicate without words. Perhaps in that dark theater we each understood that life is a battle for which none of us is ever completely prepared, that we suffer disappointments with ourselves and with each other, but that the striving transcends even our failures and our disappointments, and that sometimes the deepest bonds are unspoken.

Father and Sons

On Saturday, April 24, 1999 inside the seventy-seven year old Lowell Memorial Auditorium, twenty miles north of Boston, more than six hundred Catholic men from the six-state New England region listened to a clarion call that penetrated to the heart of all that it means to be "sons of our heavenly Father."

The event was the second New England Catholic Men's Conference, sponsored by the eleven dioceses of New England. Fittingly, months before the dawning of a new millennium, during a year consecrated to "God The Father," the glory of fatherhood and the true meaning of what it means to be a son were proclaimed boldly and without restraint.

Who are these sons, anyway, and what is this fatherhood all about? The sons are every man who has been called by name by his heavenly Father before the beginning of time. Many of them are athletes, former athletes, coaches and former coaches. Countless numbers among them are fathers themselves. All are sons. Most are husbands, but all are brothers, called to the most sacred brotherhood: a universal team of men using their gifts of manhood and masculinity to build a global society that is one with the Trinity: Father, Son and Holy Spirit.

Throughout the day, as I listened to and spoke with many men, it became clear that the theme of the conference embodied the ultimate team concept—men fighting together to win, all members of God the Father's eternal team. It struck me that I should have learned long ago that in sports and in life, all play for God the Father. He is our supreme coach and mentor.

The New England Catholic Men's Conference provided an opportunity for Catholic men to bond in union with the Father. It was a time to celebrate gender as a unique blessing; a chance and reminder to ponder the example of St. Joseph; but most of all, it was an occasion to draw strength from the fellowship grounded in God's truth.

The value of sacrifice, of commitment and perseverance, of overcoming obstacles and fighting through pain, and, of course, courage, can be taught and learned through athletics. Midway through the conference, Father Phillip Merdinger spoke about the hardest battle many men, athletes or non-athletes, will ever fight.

Father Merdinger is the founder of the Brotherhood of Hope, a public association of the faithful in the Archdiocese of Boston. It is headquartered in Somerville, only a few miles from Boston. Just before lunch, Father Merdinger spoke of the tremendous courage it takes for men to begin to understand the mystery of God the Father's love.

"All men—married men, single men, priests and religious brothers—are called to be fathers. As a man, you are a father because deep in your hearts there is a yearning to be a father, to care for others, to put things right and to exercise paternal instinct," he said.

At an even deeper level, Father Merdinger explained that all men hunger for the approval of God the Father. "I need to know that my heavenly Father approves of me, and I need to hear my heavenly Father say, 'Yes, you are my son. I love you!' "

Father Merdinger could have been the apostle Philip, speaking about the desire in the hearts of each of us, when he asked Jesus: "Show us the Father and we shall be satisfied" (John 14:8).

To come to know the Father's love, we must have the courage to take a hard look at the past and to examine, under a microscope, wounds that have been festering for years.

For men who have suffered pain in their relationships with their earthly fathers, God the Father is a foreboding, distant figure. To break down that wall and to experience the strength that only comes from being sons of our heavenly Father, a preliminary step is necessary. "We first must come to reconciliation with our own fathers, our earthly fathers," said Father Merdinger.

For scores of men, that means facing rejection, coldness, indifference, abandonment, abuse and coming to grips with deep scars, pain that begins in the heart and extends to the soul. To illustrate this point, Father Merdinger spoke about the suffering he experienced in his relationship with his own father, a sullen man who never expressed love to those closest to him. As a result, Father Merdinger said he never received the paternal love and acceptance that he craved from his dad.

"I had a hole in my heart," he said. "I was hurt and very angry for many years. It took a long time for me to experience reconciliation."

Father Merdinger said that he has spoken with many men who have experienced empty, isolated feelings because their relationship with their fathers lacked fulfillment. Unsatisfying paternal relations can trigger anger which begins as a brush fire and spreads into a raging inferno. To experience freedom and the promise of abundant life, the problem must be faced head on. Running away does not help; in fact, it hurts. Trying to escape negative feelings often leads men to seek comfort through addictions and to repeat the paternal pattern by failing at their responsibilities as husbands and fathers.

"We must be reconciled to our earthly fathers," he said. "Then we can open the door to a relationship with our heavenly Father. There is great fruitfulness in doing that because only then can we stand up and truly be fathers ourselves."

The words were received with enthusiasm.

"I never realized the concept of fatherhood was so broad," one man said.

"My father is to blame for a lot of things," said another.

"I have waited my whole life to hear what he said today. Now, I know why I have felt so trapped," a third man said.

"My own father divided himself in parts: how he acted at work, in social circles, and at home," said a fourth.

Sixteen priests heard confessions after Father Merdinger's talk.

Earlier in the day, the late Bishop John McNamara, Auxiliary Bishop of the Boston Archdiocese, spoke about fatherhood being broken by the prevailing culture. Fathers, as portrayed by popular television, are characterized as unnecessary, undesirable and even incompetent. Our country has become

'Fatherless America,'" he said. "The Catholic response to the cultural assault on fatherhood is our number one challenge."

"As men are made in the image and likeness of God," the bishop said, "it is our nature to be in communities of love, a reflection of the Holy Trinity. That means making Jesus, the perfect image of the Father, central and totally integrated into our lives."

Bishop McNamara, a Navy chaplain for twenty-six years who served in Vietnam and retired from the military as a Rear Admiral and Chief of Chaplains, told stories about Marine and Navy heroes whose understanding of the meaning of fatherhood and brotherhood motivated them "to lay down their lives for others."

He praised the Founders of America, including Presidents George Washington and Abraham Lincoln, "who were very much aware of the power, presence and wonder of God."

"We must love as Christ has loved," said the bishop, "and if we do that, the threat of a Fatherless America will meet defeat."

Mike Ruth was the next speaker. He is a former Boston College football great and recipient of the Outland Trophy, an honor given each year to the top college football lineman in the country.

Ruth spoke about "traps" such as drugs, gambling, sex, work, alcohol, lust for money, prestige and power that prevent men from hearing God's word and clinging to it.

As a youth, he faced many difficulties, including the divorce of his parents. He said the story of Our Lady appearing to three children at Fatima in 1917 changed his life. After reading the story, he went to the library and looked up the actual newspaper accounts of the apparitions.

Ruth, who is married and is the father of four, said Christ is his "strength" and his "treasure." He also talked about being the leader of his family based on rock-solid fidelity—total faithfulness—in mind, body and spirit to your spouse. He said that only by surrendering to God can we honor our marriage vows and truly be men of God.

"When we accept Christ in our hearts, He is going to do big things in us," said Ruth.

The former 285-pound nose tackle played for the New England Patriots, but had his pro football career cut short by a series of injuries. He called Catholic fellowship the most exalted form of team. "We need fellowships of real men, not wimpy men," bellowed Ruth. "I don't have time for wimpy men."

Only one woman attended the conference—Claudia Combs, a reporter for the Lowell Sun.

"I love the men's movement," she said. "It is fostering Christ-like love within men so they can be the husbands and fathers they are called to be."

The glory of the men's movement is God the Father in whom all father and son relationships become healed and whole. Only in Him, does the significance of all that it means to be sons of our heavenly Father become fulfilled.

Walter Carew, Sr.

The Eternal Metaphor

It should have come as no surprise that during his 1999 visit to America, Pope John Paul II used a sports theme to challenge the youth of the United States.

After all, the Pope has been an expert skier, mountain climber and rugged outdoorsman.

Speaking before an audience of 20,000 at the Keil Center in St. Louis, the Pope said, "We are here where many people train long and hard to compete in different sports. Today, this impressive stadium has become another kind of training ground—not for hockey, soccer or basketball, but for that training that will help you to live your faith in Jesus more decisively.

"This is the 'training in devotion' that Saint Paul is referring to—the training that makes it possible for you to give yourselves without reservation to the Lord and to the work that He calls you to do."

In his *First Letter to the Corinthians* (9:24-27), Saint Paul issued a similar challenge to the early Christians. "You know that while all the runners in the stadium take part in the race, the award goes to one man. In that case, run to win. Athletes deny themselves all sorts of things. They do this to win a crown of leaves that withers, but we a crown that is imperishable.

"I do not run like a man who loses sight of the finish line. I do not fight as if I were shadowboxing. What I do is discipline my own body and master it, for fear that after having preached to others I myself should be rejected."

How many athletes and coaches understand the potential of athletics to mirror the earthly battle for eternal life? Or how many realize that lessons learned from sports are analogous to our pilgrim journeys of faith? Obviously, the Holy Father learned that lesson many years ago, probably around the time he and his Polish countrymen battled with Nazi Germany. Certainly, Pope John Paul II learned that lesson years before he helped to bring about the destruction of the Berlin Wall and the fall of Communism.

Without the transcendent potential of athletics to reflect a greater good, sports is simply an earthly endeavor with temporal rewards. Beyond the fleeting compensations of the here and now, sports are hardly more than a hill of beans—simply recreation, like so many endeavors.

However, plug in the infinite dimension. Speak about the human soul and characterize athletes and coaches as being made in the image of God, and sports become transformed into the realms of the eternal and the imperishable.

Despite his flaws, my dad—the late Coach Walter Carew—understood that athletic competition has the potential to reflect more, that sports can be used as a metaphor to help examine life's more perplexing questions. To him, the condition of an athlete's soul was every bit as important as the development of the body.

As a head football coach, each year he sent a letter to every candidate for the high school football team. Here is a sample of one letter. It is dated August 21, 1965. After my father died, my mom pulled it out and gave it to me, along with his practice schedules, play book and other memorabilia from his career as a high school football coach.

Instead of a regular, formal greeting, like "Dear Football Candidate," Dad addressed his football players with two words:

"GUNG HO!!!"

Here is the rest of the letter he wrote on a late summer day in 1965 almost thirty-five years ago:

"Football is the finest game in the world. This is true because football challenges you in three meaningful areas: physical, intellectual and moral. In short, it helps to make a complete man of you.

If you want to participate in this highly significant experience, report to the student lounge on Monday, August 30th, at 9:30 A.M. for a physical examination. No one is allowed to practice without a physical.

We will begin our practice sessions right after the exams. Double sessions will be in order until school opens the following week. Football equipment will be issued on Friday morning, August 27, and Saturday morning, August 28, at 9:00 A.M.

GUNG HO!!! Which means, among other things, the true measure of a man is the greatness of his soul.

Sincerely,

Coach Carew"

Here I must add a brief background sketch to explain my father's signature phrase, "Gung Ho." It was his favorite catch phrase. For him, it had religious, athletic and military significance: persevering, at all cost, along our pilgrimages of faith; loving your teammates, sacrificing for the greater good of the team, dying to self; and overcoming all obstacles, in football, in life and in war, as he and his fellow soldiers did while fighting in the Battle of the Bulge during World War II. Over the years, when he greeted one of his former players, instead of saying, "Hello," he often just said, "Gung Ho," and followed the salutation with a salute.

"Late have I loved thee" – St. Augustine. As a high school athlete, I was exposed to the deeper aspects of competitive athletics through him, my coach and father. At the time, I did not appreciate the opportunity I had, at such a young age, to learn about truths that I would need for the rest of my life. In fact, I blocked out what my dad tried to teach me, my teammates, and every high school football player who ever played for him.

At the time, I did not want to hear the Gospel of Jesus Christ being taught on a football field. I did not want to hear about the redemptive value of suffering. Nor did I want to listen to talk about self-sacrifice, discipline and the importance of mastering a weak, fallen nature. Some of my teammates got the message. Others did not. Thank God, I finally got it, but it was years after my athletic career was over.

Better late than never. That's what I say today, although I realize I still have bundles to learn. And always will. My natural inclination is to avoid what is unpleasant, to seek the path of least resistance. Every day, however, I pick up a little bit more of all that my father taught. It comes in trickles, mostly during difficult times.

Life is filled with mysteries. As a high school athlete I was unreachable. Why? Probably a combination of things. Certainly, I had shortcomings. But another factor was that my father, who gave unconditional love to my teammates, could not give it to me. I know my father loved us, but he kept a cap on his feelings. When his football teams lost, he closed the bedroom door and sulked for hours. When we passed the room, we tiptoed. And when we failed him, we were greeted with a cold silence. And so in many ways, I spent a lot of time tiptoeing past my father.

No one, however, including me, ever questioned what motivated my dad, the coach, the teacher. It was the Gospel message of Jesus Christ, and more specifically, the deposit of faith taught by the Catholic Church. As for his vocation as a teacher-coach, he called it "a sacred trust" and "a privileged opportunity." Because of the influence a coach can have on an athlete, my dad often said: "Coaching is the greatest profession in the world." He also believed the purest form of athletic competition is found at the high school level.

It amazes me that a mere game—football—could be a repository where truths about the essence of man and his eternal destiny can be uncovered, taught and learned. Even more astounding is the fact that my father worked at a public school where a large percentage of the student-athletes were not Catholic.

Later, after he came out of retirement, he coached football at St. Bernard's Catholic high school in Fitchburg, Massachusetts. I spotted the ad for a head football coach in the newspaper and urged him to apply. He hesitated, but at last he did. It was a wonderful four-year experience for him. He loved the school and the athletes, and they loved him, too. He quickly developed a deep and lasting friendship with the headmaster, the late Father Richard Hennigan.

Once he took the job, he threw all caution to the wind. He no longer muffled language that previously would have sounded too Catholic, too orthodox. His pre-game preparations climaxed at a team Mass, followed by prayers and reflections on how even football matters deeply in the context of the mystery of faith. All of what we do in this life, I have come to learn—even playing or coaching football, counts both in time and in eternity.

I thought of my father as I watched and listened to the Holy Father during his address at the Keil Center.

"I am told that there was much excitement in St. Louis during the recent baseball season, when two great players [Mark McGwire and Sammy Sosa] were competing to break the home run record," the pope told his audience. "You can feel the same great enthusiasm as you train for a different goal—the goal of following Christ, the goal of bringing his message to the world. This is the time of your 'training', of your physical, intellectual, emotional, and spiritual development."

Addressing the youth in St. Louis, the Holy Father repeatedly used a sports theme to pound home the Gospel message of Christ.

"But this does not mean that you can put off until later your meeting with Christ and your sharing in the Church's mission. Even though you are young, the time for action is now! Jesus does not have contempt for your youth. He does not set you aside for a later time when you will be older and your training will be complete. Your training will never be finished. Christians are always in training. You are ready for what Christ wants of you now. He wants you—all of you—to be light to the world, as only young people can be light. It is time to let your light shine!"

Pope John Paul II met briefly with McGwire, and the all-time, single season, major league baseball home run king knelt and kissed the Holy Father's ring.

My father, like McGwire and so many others, loved and revered the Holy Father, calling him "the greatest man of our lifetime." And he often made the prediction that one day the Polish-born pontiff would be known as "John Paul The Great."

At the end of my dad's life, this once robust man who had such a keen mind, became physically feeble and mentally disoriented. He shuffled when he walked and loss of memory left him confused and frustrated. Every day became a personal battle; different than any he had fought before, yet maybe the toughest. It broke my heart to watch him deteriorate as a combination of physical ailments sapped the life right out of him.

As his condition worsened, his Catholic faith sustained him. He constantly clutched a rosary and carried it to bed. Although he had lost the ability to read, he carried a book *Crossing The Threshold Of Hope*, written by Pope John Paul II, everywhere. It was never out of his sight. He even lugged it to the bathroom with him. Sometimes he held it right side up; at other times, he squeezed it with both his hands, upside-down.

After he died, my mother gave the book to me. She also gave me a white "Army Football" cap that was given to him by my brother-in-law, Lawrence Kenney, during a trip to West Point. The trip was highlighted by a parade in the morning followed by an Army versus Boston College football game at Michie Stadium. My father wore that cap every day at the Veterans

Hospital in Bedford, Massachusetts, where he spent the last month of his life and where he died.

Only my wife and my mother understand how much I cherish that hat. It has begun to fade, but I will never throw it away. I wear it to church, to work, to ball games, when I go on errands and sometimes I even wear it when I'm writing.

I wish every boy who ever played football for my dad could have seen him fighting to hang onto the Holy Father's book during "the fourth quarter" of his life. If they had, his exhortation: "Don't fumble, no matter what. Hang onto the football with both hands. Let no one or anything stop you. Fight all the way into the end zone!" would have been seen in the light of what St. Paul and Pope John Paul II meant when they spoke about "winning an imperishable crown."

Finally, when I think about my father, I am reminded of the words from Paul's *Second Letter to Timothy* (4:6-8): "I for my part am already being poured out like a libation. The time of my dissolution is near. I have fought the good fight, I have finished the race, I have kept the faith. From now on a merited crown awaits me; on that day the Lord, just judge that he is, will award it to me—and not only to me, but to all who have looked to his appearing with eager longing."

My eager longing continues, but my father's is over. He is still one up on me.